D1226795

THE UNKNOWN NOËL

THE UNKNOWN

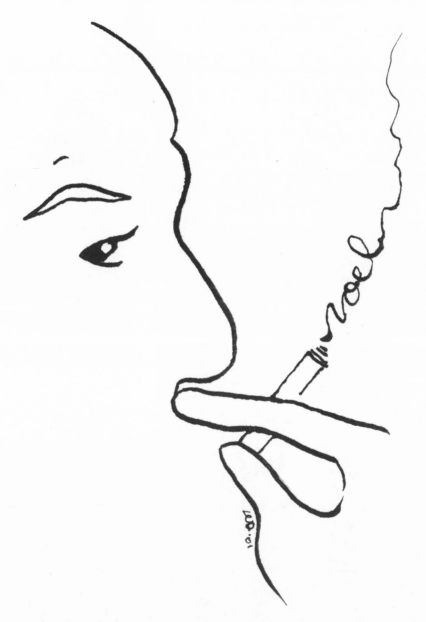

NOËL

New Writing from the Noël Coward Archive

EDITED AND ANNOTATED BY
BARRY DAY

SECOND OPINION, INC.

First published by Second Opinion, Inc. in October 2001

All new Noël Coward material © The Noël Coward Estate 2001.

Format and linking commentary © Barry Day 2001

Lyrics quoted are from *Noël Coward: The Complete Lyrics* (1998),
The Overlook Press. Used by permission.

EDITOR'S NOTE:
With the exception of the 1940 radio broadcast, and the introduction to Mander &
Mitchenson's *Musical Comedy* (1969), there is no indication in the Archive that any of
the other material in this collection was ever published or broadcast—for the obvious
reason that it was by its nature incomplete in one way or another. If I have accidentally
overlooked any attributions, I shall be glad to acknowledge them in any subsequent
editions of this book.

PHOTO CREDITS:
Certain of the photographs used come from collections and are used by permission—
Museum of the City of New York (p. 25); The New York Public Library of the
Performing Arts, Billy Rose Theatre Collection [Vandamm Theatre Photograph
Collection] (p. 32-33, 40, 45); The Mander & Mitchenson Theatre Collection
(p. 101); Geoffrey Johnson private collection (p. 47, 140, 156-157). The remainder
come from the Coward Archive.

Book design and type formatting by Bernard Schleifer
Title page illustration by Lynne Carey
Noël Coward graphic by Identica

Printed in the United States of America
ISBN 0-9537659-4-6

DEDICATED TO THE IRREPLACEABLE

JOAN HIRST

. . . A GETTER-ON-ER, A BUCKER-UP-ER . . .
AND A REAL LADY

CONTENTS

PREFACE

With Noël's centenary upon us, I asked my friend and colleague, Barry Day to help me review the contents of the Coward Archive. To be honest, since Coley and I sorted and packed up Noël's vast store of papers soon after his death in 1973, I hadn't had the heart to go through them in any organised way.

Oh, of course I knew the vault contained original manuscripts of many of the plays and hundreds of letters from anybody who was anybody in the first seventy years of the twentieth century. But what was in those dozens of folders and notebooks, some of them dating back to his teenage years?

The answer was a whole miscellany of short stories, verse, song lyrics, essays, notes on contemporaries, scenes from unfinished plays, lines that might one day find a place in plays . . . in short, a private and privileged glimpse into the mind of a man whose lifelong compulsion was to *write*.

Much of the material took shape before our eyes. Here was the draft script of a musical called *Later Than Spring* that would be developed into *Sail Away* . . . there was another called *Hoi Polloi* that would be re-shaped into *Ace of Clubs*, a show in which I was to star.

Here were lyrics cut from shows . . . there were the more familiar ones with notations in Noël's distinctive spidery writing, changing a word here, a phrase there, until they became the songs we know by heart.

It was a fascinating and for me a very moving experience. And one thing became very clear. It was an experience every Noël Coward fan would have liked to share.

This anthology of previously unpublished writings is our attempt to let you do just that. Barry has grouped the material and his commentary sets it in context.

So, for all of you who would like to hear The Master's voice once more . . .

Graham Payn
Les Avants
2001

THE BOY ACTOR

I can remember. I can remember,
The months of November and December,
Although climatically cold and damp,
Meant more to me than Aladdin's lamp.
I see myself, having got a job,
Walking on wings along the Strand,
Uncertain whether to laugh or sob
And clutching tightly my mother's hand.
I never cared who scored the goal
Or which side won the silver cup,
I never learned to bat or bowl
But I heard the curtain going up

("The Boy Actor")

VIOLET COWARD WAS THE ARCHETYPAL "STAGE MOTHER" AND IT WAS TO HER hand the young Noël was firmly attached in his early theatrical years.

Beginning with the auspicious role of Prince Mussel in the 1911 production of the children's play, *The Goldfish*, he was ceaselessly working or in search of work—in common with hundreds of other hopeful mites (and their mothers) . . .

THE DRESS REHEARSAL

"I wonder how long Baby will be?"

Mrs. Blabbin rose and opened the door—a noise of far off screaming was wafted along the passage. She came back and sat down with a sigh. "Only doing the finale of the Palace scene."

"My Minnie's not in that," cried a long thin woman, getting up hurriedly and going to the door.

"For Heaven's sake, don't keep 'hopening and shutting the door," murmured Mrs. Delamere, who was ladylike first and literate afterwards.

"Brenda won't let her come up till they've finished—I know her of old—Gracie was here in *Cinderella* last year."

"Baby's never played Panto before," remarked Mrs. Blabbin with slight superiority, "All this is quite new to us."

The three women sighed faintly.

"I wish he'd give Minnie more of a chance."

"Well, Mrs. Peach—I always have said of all the heartrending professions. When Baby just went on, my husband was furious "What will everyone say?" he said. And I said "Who *cares* what they say? The child 'as talent, that's plain to any eye." "But think," he said "of the ups and downs." And I said, "My baby's got talent and she'll win through" and he said . . . ."

Here Mrs. Delamere cut short her discourse by sneezing loudly.

"The dressing rooms here aren't nearly as warm as the Apollyon. Gracie was there with *Mr. Teetle* and what a hit she made—you would have laughed. I bought a book to put her notices in and it wasn't big enough so I had to get another—there, wasn't that funny . . .?"

"I never keep Baby's notices now," remarked Mrs. Blabbin with emphasis. "After all . . ."

"Brenda sent for Minnie last Thursday," said Mrs. Peach, "just after she'd signed the contract for this—to play lead in a sketch with Dolola—you know, the snake charmer woman."

"I wouldn't let Baby work with a snake charmer," said Mrs. Blabbin firmly.

"Nasty dangerous beasts . . ."

"All their fangs would be drawn, of course," said Mrs. Pearl.

"Gracie was to be the daughter of a Princess and do her Eastern dance, which she changed, you know, the one with cymbals she did at the audition . . .?"

"I only wish Brandon'd give Minnie more point work," sighed Mrs. Delamere, "Esperanza said her instep was like an arch . . ."

"Anyhow, it's disgraceful keeping the poor kids up so late. They let Gracie off quite early every night rehearsing for *Puss* in Manchester.

"Well," remarked Mrs. Blabbin with an air of pained finality, "if Baby doesn't get home soon, her father will be so furious he'll come down and give Brandon a good telling off. He was furious at her going into Panto at all—but as I said, "My baby's got talent and I said . . ."

(1921)

*   *   *   *

In retrospect, Noël was in no doubt that he—in common with just about every so-called 'child prodigy' must have presented a gruesome spectacle to anyone of a sensitive disposition. "Perhaps my lack of self-consciousness and my youth mitigated a little the horror of the situation, but I am certain that could my adult self have been present . . . he would have crept out, at the first coy gurgle, and been mercifully sick outside."

THE CHILD PRODIGY

An infant prodigy of nine
Is shoved upon the stage in white.
She starts off in a dismal whine
About a Dark and Stormy night,
A burglar whose heart is true,
Despite his wicked looking face!
And what a little child can do
To save her Mama's jewel case!
This may bring tears to every eye.
It does not set my heart on fire
I'd like to stand serenely by
And watch that Horrid child expire!

(From "Concert Types"— 1 9 1 7)

*   *   *   *

In 1911 Noël was given his first professional part as The Page by actor-manager, Sir Charles Hawtrey (1858-1923) in a play called The Great Name. *From there he went straight into Hawtrey's* Where the Rainbow Ends, *a children's play that for a while rivaled* Peter Pan *in popularity.*

In charge of the ballet was the formidable Miss Italia Conti. Miss Conti also specialised in supplying children for any and all London theatrical productions and decided to 'appropriate' the young Noël for subsequent shows. In later years she would often claim credit for her 'pupil's' success but relations between these two independent personalities were, it seems, strained at best. The lady's suggestion that he might care to play the part of a hyena was one that he never forgot. . .

ODE TO ITALIA CONTI

Oh, Italia, with thy face so pale
Why must you float about the Stalls
Where Mr. Hawtrey sits?
Dost think that passing thus thou wilt prevail
Upon him to cut out the finest bits

Which we poor principals in our parts must speak?
We often hear the hapless ballet tremble
When they're corrected by your raucous squeak.

To principals you like not you will serve
Out contracts in which cheek and guile are blended
And then you have the most appalling nerve
To say they must be yours till world is ended.
In vain you've tried to lure us to your classes—
We are not such unmitigated asses.

(1921)

*   *   *   *

Juvenile theatre provided the young Noël with his initiation into the battle of the sexes—the battle being for the best parts. It was in this dusty arena that he learned to recognise the devious Eve lurking beneath the fluttering eyelash and the angelic voice—an insight that was to serve him well in dealing with leading ladies for the next fifty years!

SOUVENIR

Whatever became of those dear little girls
I used to dislike so much?
I can see them now as they came to tea
Simpering slightly, aware of me
Not as a friend, another child,
But as someone later to be beguiled
With roguish giggles and tossing of curls.
They were ready to scream at a touch.
Whatever became of those dear little girls
I used to dislike so much?

But there was one notable exception. For many of those childhood years his closest friend was a fellow child actor, Esmé Wynne.

They gave each other pet names. Noël was "Poj" and Esmé was 'Stoj'. They played and plotted together in their own private world.

They also wrote plays together under the combined nom de plume *of 'Esnomel' and by 1917 even had a couple of them professionally staged.*

But perhaps the most affecting piece of prose they produced between them was the binding contract that defined their friendship . . .

RULES OF PALSHIP BETWEEN ESME WYNNE AND NOEL COWARD

1. We must not tease one another and if we begin we must stop directly we are asked.

2. We must take it in turns to go and see one another and if one goes twice running to the other's house, the other must do the same afterwards.

3. We must *never* split on one another even if the PALSHIP is dissolved and we must hold all confidences sacred.

4. We must share all profits in any transaction made together, however slight the help of the other may be. Profits are excluded from any expenses incurred during the said transaction.

5. In case of serious quarrel a week or a fortnight may be taken to think things over before abolishing the PALSHIP.

6. If one hits the other either in anger or fun, he must allow the other to hit back. Any other offence must be paid for.

7. We must stick up for each other against anyone or anything, and stand by each other in all danger.

8. We must tell each other all secrets concerned with ourselves, other confidences may be held sacred even from one another.

9. We must not talk RELIGION unless it is inevitable.

10. When writing to mutual friends we must tell each other, we must also tell each other what we have said in the letter.

11. We must swear by <u>"HONOUR AS A PAL"</u> and hold it <u>THE</u> most sacred of bonds in the world.

12. We must tell each other what we think about the other's appearance or behaviour.

13. We must go straight to one another in case of mischief being made and believe NOTHING unless it comes from the other's own lips.

14. NO ONE, not even our Parents, may keep us from one another.

15. If any other rules are formed or thought of, they must be added (with the consent of both) at the end of this document.

16. <u>NO OTHER PERSON</u> may be admitted into our PALSHIP or SECRETS.

SIGNATURE OF BOTH

Dated August the 11th 1915_____

                    Esmé Wynne   Noël Coward

Second only to Violet Coward, Esmé was to be the most important influence in Noël's professional life—until the arrival of Gertrude Alexandra Dagmar Lawrence-Klasen . . .

TOURING DAYS

Touring days, touring days,
What ages it seems to be
Since the landlady at Norwich
Served a mouse up in the porridge,
And a beetle in the morning tea . . .
Those wonderful touring days

("Touring Days")

THE NATIONAL THEATRICAL TOUR WAS A PHENOMENON OF BOTH BRITISH AND American show business for the first half of the last century — until the movies arrived, full of sound and then colour and later television, which ended its run by closing most of the theatres and keeping its audience glued to their fireside armchairs.

No self-respecting Hollywood film on the subject was without a montage of train wheels turning, whistles shrieking and the names of destinations hurtling past the viewer.

The British version was predictably more mundane but for the performers there were still endless vistas of Sunday morning train calls, as the cast moved from one dull town to another that looked precisely the same . . . lugging shabby suitcases up flights of narrow stairs in back street boarding houses under the eagle eye of identical shrewish landladies, who basically disapproved of 'theatricals'. All this in the name of—The Theatre.

As a young actor Noël put in his time 'on the road', though in his case, he was never forced to face the downward spiral so many of his colleagues experienced of smaller and smaller towns and an ever lower place on the bill. Nonetheless, he observed it all acutely and found time to write about it . . . the hopes, the fears, and the performances that go on before the curtain goes up . . .

THE RISING STAR

‘LAST NIGHT AT THE ORIEL NETTIE GRAY’S PART WAS TAKEN UP AT SHORT NOTICE BY DODY FARRANT, WHO PROVED HERSELF NOT ONLY TO BE A FINE ACTRESS BUT A BRILLIANT SINGER AND A DELIGHTFUL DANCER—BRAVO!’

“I think she’s very good considering . . .”

“Considering—what?”

“Well, she went on at half a day’s warning . . .”

“Don’t be funny, she’s been rehearsing for *weeks*”

“Yes, but only with the other understudies—of course she can’t work the numbers but her dialogue isn’t bad.”

“Except for the American accent. More like Wapping, I should say.”

“O, shut up, Cissie—you’re too sharp to live. Lend me your eye black and don’t talk so much. I think she’s damn fine—except for the last act. Of course, she can’t *dance* but still . . .”

“That’s what *i* say. There are lots of others who could have done it much better.”

“It’s a jolly fat part.”

“Yes, but quite actor proof—everybody feeds her all the time and, of course, I think she’s too common in it but still . . .”

“Not exactly *common*, dear, but she ’asn’t the refinement that Nettie has . . .”

“I don’t mind the way she does the part—after all, she only has to imitate Nettie all the time and copy all her bits of business. What I object to is all this in the press. I suppose her man does it for her . . .”

“I shouldn’t think he’s influential enough . . .”

“I like him—he’s funny, makes me pass out . . .”

“I think he’s a silly young swine. I wish he’d use his influence and make her take her hair off her face—she looks like a blasted Pekinese. And why in God’s name don’t they let her have decent clothes? After all, if you can’t dance or sing, you ought to *look* well anyhow. . .”

“I wouldn’t go so far as to say she couldn’t *sing*, dear. The trouble is that the numbers are too high for her—that’s why she’s flat all the time.”

“Well, I think she’s very good, dear, if only she wouldn’t . . .”

“Look out, Cissie. . .”

“Oh, Dody, dear, you were wonderful! We were just saying . . .”

“Thank God an English girl has made good. I was just saying to

Helen—'Helen', I said 'that girl's a second Gertie Millar'—didn't I, Helen?"

"Yes, darling, you did. I am so glad, Dody, dear—we always said you'd click!"

"Darling, how did you manage that gorgeous American accent—it's marvellous . . ."

". . . of course, I think you sing 'Doll Dream' better than Nettie—she's so apt to get flat. And that awful frock she has! Yours is fifty times better—so simple . . ."

"Well, all I can say is you're amazing—you're absolutely made . . ."

"Of course, where you score is your dancing. I was only saying just now . . ."

(1922)

*   *   *   *

But for every star in the ascendant there were always several on the way down the theatrical firmament. For every Dody Farrant there were a dozen Babsies.

WHEN BABSIE GOT THE BIRD

Babsie's on the stage. She's only forty!
Babsie's got a grown up girl and boy -
She tries her very hardest to be naughty
And thinks it looks alluring to be coy
Babsie's sung in all the halls round London West
She still hopes that in time she'll reach them
From what I know about her
I rather strongly doubt her
Ability to give them what is best.

Then poor old Babs'll get the bird again,
The Bird again once more
And for a week or two she won't be heard of again
But she won't be off for long, you may be sure.
Then one fine day she will appear again
At some outlandish place, you bet
And when we're dead and gone,
As the years go rolling on, Babsie still the bird will get.
Babsie's first engagement was a failure,

Babsie's second also was a frost.
Babsie toured for years in South Australia
With a song, the theme of which she always lost.
Once she sang it in a Nature Village
In the middle of the vast Australian scrub.
She said, 'It seems to strike me
That these people don't quite like me."
Another thing that struck her was a club.

Then poor old Babsie got the bird again,
The bird again much worse.
I don't think that song e'er will be heard,
They had to fetch a doctor and a nurse
But soon Babsie got all right again
And lately she's been singing quite a lot
And even when I'm dead,
I'm sure I'll hear it said
That Babs again the bird has got.

*   *   *   *

*At a lower level in the theatrical food chain was 'Rep'—the semi-permanent repertory company that inhabited a permanent theatre in a provincial town and put on—as the name suggests—a 'repertory' of shows designed to please a regular local audience. One week—*Twelfth Night. *The next—*Arsenic and Old Lace. *One week you play the lead; the next you're carrying a spear. But at least, you're acting, laddie.*

REPERTORY WORK

Vivien Bailey was new to repertory work. Her past experience embraced farce, pantomime, musical comedy and one drama—but this rush of new parts every week was enchanting. What wonderful training it would be. The company seemed nice, too—perhaps a little gloomy but still the town wasn't a particularly bright spot.

John Randolph—usual juvenile, occasional character—seemed the most light-hearted of the bunch. He'd been with the management nearly two years. Violet Craig told Vivien that he'd had a terrible affair with Effie Grainger, the red haired girl who was playing 'Winka' on Monday. It had lasted a long time. Vivien regarded the temperamental Effie across the stage with wonder. How could she go on in the same company after her affair with the principal man was over and everybody knew it and discussed it—horrible!

Vivien shuddered and again tried to master her first role in *The Knight of the Burning Pestle*. She read steadily through all the parts in the little standard edition of the play. Some of the lines had been crossed out by the tender-minded management as being a little too strong even for repertory. Those Elizabethans must have been objectionable and dirty.

John Randolph finished his scene and came and sat down by her. He had a nice, attractive speaking voice and was well mannered. They conversed amiably and discovered one another's favourite books. John asked if her digs were comfortable and that, if not, he knew of a jolly good address in Paradise Street—No. 18. Vivien laughed because that happened to be her address. John also laughed, because that also happened to be his.

The first few weeks of the season passed uneventfully. Vivien played several parts with a certain amount of success and every night she and John used to travel home in the tram together. They bade one another charming goodnights on reaching their digs and parted, he to his first floor front and she to her ground floor back.

To Vivien's surprise he made no effort at intimacy with her. Judging from talk in the dressing room, this was unlike his usual behaviour. Vivien felt rather slighted. She would have liked a little more of his companionship.

Effie Grainger continued to play good parts—mostly love scenes with John—entirely unmoved. Vivien marvelled at her control. Everyone said she was still in love with him. How could she!

One morning Vivien met John in Boot's when she was changing her library book and asked her to lunch with him at Fuller's. In the middle of lunch he gave her a slightly sad look:

"I wonder why we don't talk to one another more?"

"Why should we?"

"Well, we're in the same digs, it seems so stupid. You sit and have your supper in lonely state every night. So do I. We might as well feed together sometimes . . ."

Vivien, on whom the loneliness had of late begun to pall somewhat, smiled—"By all means, let's. We can hear one another rehearse our parts." That night after the show John renewed his invitation.

"Come up and have supper with me tonight and I'll feed with you tomorrow night in return."

Vivien agreed and after she'd taken off her hat and coat she went upstairs and knocked on his door. He had put on a dark jacket and looked very nice in it. There was cold beef and tomatoes and potato salad and pineapple and custard for supper. They talked over it and were awfully nice companions for one another. Then after, when they had drawn up two rather shiny armchairs to the fire, Vivien began to realise the charm of atmosphere. The memories of dreary evenings by herself recurred in odious comparison to this—and there was wonderful Romance in the furniture of a front room. The hideous cosiness of it was most attractive. The fire crackled and the incandescent gas mantle gave occasional gentle 'pops', as though it was glad to be alive and burning.

She looked at the pictures—'Daddy's Girl', 'Ventnor Pier' in a green plush frame, those terrible china shepherdesses on the mantlepiece and the wilting aspidistra in a pink pot in front of the window. It was all very warm and comfortable. She saw John looking at her intently and then suddenly, without any warning she gave in. There would be a wonderful thrill in loving somebody very much in these surroundings. John leaned forward and caught her hands. Then he kissed her wonderfully. His arms were very strong and the smell of his smoking jacket was adorable. They went on for ages, those kisses. After all, she was alone in the world. It didn't really matter . . .

About eighteen months later at the beginning of the Autumn season a new girl came up to Vivien at rehearsal—she was engaged for various character parts—and asked what John Randolph was like. Two or three other women standing near nudged her and trod on her foot because she was so tactless. Later on they explained why. The new girl was impressed but surprised.

"But how can she go on acting in the same company with him after all . . .?"

"Why shouldn't she—what does it matter?"

John Randolph smiled to himself as he heard the new girl clattering about in the ground floor flat. He was feeling very weary. Repertory was wearing him out. After all, he *had* been on the stage for fifty years now . . .

(1922)

*   *   *   *

. . . Still, it's all worth it, when you know there's an audience out there, sitting there with bated breath, hanging on your every move. There is an audience out there, isn't there?

THEATRE PARTY

"There can be few things more embarrassing for a delicately nurtured girl", reflected Eleanor Satterwhite pensively, "than to have to wait unattended in a public place while one's gentleman escort palpably lingers in the lavatory, but doubtless when one has attained years of comparative discretion these little errors of taste on Nature's part become less troublesome. "

She regarded the large hall of Claridge's Hotel somewhat wearily and sighed. "It is also unfortunate," she continued to herself, "that one's sense of dignity impels one to remain standing when it would be infinitely more comfortable to sit down but to sit down in a hotel lounge invariably gives me the sensation of being a new housemaid sitting on a tin trunk at Waterloo and there could indeed be no more dreary precedent than that with which to start an evening ostensibly devoted to unalloyed pleasure."

Presently Harry Lightfoot rejoined her, his faultless evening dress concealed by his still more faultless coat with a suspicion of velvet at the collar and a carefully knotted white silk scarf enhanced by a tasteful monogram in black. As he steered the luxurious Rolls-Royce coupé through the turmoil of traffic in Piccadilly she noticed with a certain thrill several silky black hairs upon his wrist in the brief space between his white glove and the sleeve of his coat and could not help but dwell for a moment upon the sensation she would derive from pressing them gently with her lips. But fearing that the gratification of this natural desire would not only appear slightly forward so early in the evening but in all probability menace the safety of the drive, she contented herself with squeezing his arm gently and enjoying to the full the play of his muscles beneath her fingers.

Upon arrival at the theatre she found herself once more doomed to a period of lonely inactivity while Harry parked the car beneath the eye of some watchful policeman. She stood in the foyer and scrutinised without enthusiasm the photographs of the play they were about to witness. "To be an actress must be an exceedingly trying profession," she thought. "For as one's emotions are assuredly useful to one only to the extent of the pleasure they give, it must therefore be heartbreaking to be forced to spill them with carefully measured reiteration night after night, thereby gradually blunting the senses until nothing but the most flagrant indelicacies can prove even faintly satisfying."

When Harry reappeared they were conducted to their box by an immaculately dressed but rather over-developed young lady smelling slightly of old clothes, who offered them chocolates, which they refused, and a programme, which they accepted, and then indicated with some hauteur a small salon at the back of the box neatly furnished with a sofa and a table and two chairs, whose privilege it was to sustain their majesties the King and Queen whenever they happened to visit the theatre.

In the course of the first act the sudden pressure of Harry's left hand upon her knee drew Eleanor's slightly languid attention from the stage and she looked at him reprovingly until, rather abashed by her expression, he turned his head unconcernedly away and inspected the Dress Circle with elaborate boredom. But his hand still remained on her knee and she could feel the warmth of it quite distinctly penetrating through her frock. "I will not attempt to hide from myself that the pressure of Harry's hand is very attractive to me," she reflected, "but whether or not to encourage further excursions so early in the evening I am at a loss to decide." Her cogitations were here cut short by Harry's leg twining itself tightly around hers and she was unable to avoid the reality that the rapidity of his breathing was only to be equalled by the beating of her own heart.

When the curtain fell on the first act they both withdrew into the small salon to enjoy the furtive privilege of a cigarette. She sat on the sofa, while Harry commented unfavourably on the few minor engravings with which the room was hung. His voice was strangely husky and both his hands were in his trouser pockets. Presently a shrill bell rang somewhere and Eleanor rose to re-enter the box but before she was able to reach the door, Harry's arms were crushing her to him and his mouth was opening on hers with forceful insistence. "It would be foolish to deny," she murmured to herself, as he bent her backwards onto the sofa, "that young men now apparently learn a tremendous lot in the navy."

As Eleanor stood before her mirror that night, thoughtfully massaging her nose with toilet cream, a slight frown puckered for an instant the smooth surface of her brow, then it vanished and she climbed into her bed with the air of one who has arrived at a satisfactory decision. "I must re-visit that excellent play alone during a matinée," she sighed drowsily. "For I feel that to attain a decently critical understanding of it a knowledge of the second act is essential."

(1922)

*   *   *   *

CHAPTER THREE

TONIGHT AT 8:30

WORLD'S RICHEST WRITERS—1932

Noël Coward	£50,000
George Bernard Shaw	£35,000
A.A. Milne	£30,000
Rudyard Kipling	£30,000

TONIGHT AT 8:30

WHEN HE USED THE TITLE *TONIGHT AT 8:30* TO LINK A SERIES OF ONE ACT plays he'd written as star vehicles for himself and Gertrude Lawrence Noël was simply appropriating a currently popular phrase to describe the excitement of the witching hour as the theatre curtain rose to reveal . . . who knew what magic?

In our more prosaic age, while the magic may still intermittently occur, the thrill of theatre-going *per se* has all but vanished. Hard to imagine the excitement generated by the expectation of seeing 'Noël and Gertie' together again.

They had been child actors together in their teens, then appeared in Noël's 1923 revue, *London Calling!*. He had set out to write his first 'book' musical, *Bitter Sweet* for her in 1929 but, as the music emerged, it became clear to both of them that her rather fragile singing voice was not up to the demands of the role of Sari. To make amends, he wrote *Private Lives* for the two of them the following year.

No reader of this book needs me to describe the plot or summarise the success of *Private Lives*. However many times the play is revived and no matter how brilliantly the roles are reconceived by other actors, the voices one hears in the theatre-of-the-mind are Noël's and Gertie's and it is their images we see, standing side by side on that hotel balcony, looking out at the Duke of Westminster's inevitable yacht.

Elyot and Amanda/Noël and Gertie. Almost as soon as they first played the parts, Noël clearly recognised that characters and actors had somehow coalesced—to the point where he could use them as subject matter for a satirical, self-mocking sketch. Whether they ever performed it in public is not known but they do so now . . .

STRICTLY PRIVATE LIVES

Gertie and Noël are discovered lying on the sofa in Private Lives *attitude. The gramophone is playing their own record. It finishes.*

NOËL: Darling, you oughtn't to have whistled just there—it sounds tinny.

GERTIE: Tinny, my foot

NOËL: I beg your pardon

GERTIE: I said—"Tinny, my foot".

NOËL: I do hope you're not going to turn out to be disagreeable.

GERTIE: I'm not in the least disagreeable, but it's silly to go on about that whistling; everybody adores that record, and they write to me from all over the country saying they particularly like the whistling—it gives a sense of intimacy.

NOËL: Intimacy, my grandmother.

GERTIE: My foot and your grandmother ought to get together.

NOËL: That would mean your having one foot in the grave.

GERTIE: Very funny. I can't imagine how you always think of those swift witty replies—it's wonderful, it is, really.

NOËL: Be quiet.

GERTIE: What!

NOËL: I said—"Be quiet".

GERTIE: You should never have written *Cavalcade*. It was a grave mistake.

NOËL: Why?

GERTIE: Because it's blown you up like a frog, a pompous National Frog.

NOËL: Look here . . .

GERTIE: You're so damned pleased with yourself.

NOËL: Pleased with myself! I should like to say one thing -

GERTIE: Sollocks, Darling—oh, Sollocks

(Two minutes pause, Noël puts on a dance record)

NOËL: Do you feel like dancing?

GERTIE: Not at all.

(They dance)

NOËL: Why are we doing this?

GERTIE: Charity.

NOËL: What charity?

GERTIE: I haven't the slightest idea, I believe it's something to do with angry old governesses.

NOËL: I thought it was a Fresh Air Fund for the waiters at the Café de Paris.

GERTIE: Anyhow, it doesn't matter, does it?

NOËL: Not a bit.

(They dance in silence for a moment or two)

A pretty thing about the financial situation.

GERTIE: Very pretty.

NOËL: Looks as though there might be a revolution among the Welsh miners.

GERTIE: You'd better write a play about it.

NOËL: *(Leaving her and stopping the gramophone)* That was rude.

GERTIE: I don't see why.

NOËL: Cigarette?

GERTIE: No.

NOËL: *(Lighting one)* Are you going to sing in your new play?

GERTIE: No

NOËL: Good.

GERTIE: How dare you say that?

NOËL: I think you left musical comedy in the *nick* of time.

GERTIE: Nick, nick, nick. What do you mean—nick?

NOËL: Your voice is not what it was.

GERTIE: Yours is, and that's what's wrong with it.

NOËL: At least I don't sing flat.

GERTIE: Meaning that I do?

NOËL: *Knowing* that you do.

GERTIE: Flat, indeed!

NOËL: *Very* flat.

GERTIE: You're insufferable.

NOËL: Darling—Sollocks!

> *(Noël goes in silence to the piano. They sing a few songs.*
> *During the last one he stops just as she is taking a top note.)*

There you are—*flat!*

> *(He bangs the note)*

(c.1930)

*   *   *   *

When Gertie died prematurely in 1952, a devastated Noël would write in his obituary for The Times *that "no one I have ever known, however brilliant and however gifted, has contributed quite what she contributed to my work."*

*In saying it, he temporarily upset another deeply affectionate relationship—with The Lunts (*ALFRED LUNT *and* LYNN FONTANNE*).*

Noël had met them on his first impoverished trip to New York in 1921. Already a couple but not yet married, they were both beginning to make their separate marks on Broadway. Noël was still a few years away from making his on either side of the Atlantic.

Their three careers were to run in parallel for the rest of their lives but it was on this first acquaintance that the bond was forged. Noël wrote three plays specifically for The Lunts but it was the first that made theatrical history. When they were all equally successful, it was determined on that first visit, Noël was to write a play in which the three of them would appear together to great acclaim.

*In 1933 he did—*Design for Living. *Gilda (Lynn), Otto (Alfred) and Leo (Noël)are all in love with each other—not to mention themselves—and no two of them can manage for long without the third.*

This somewhat incestuous closeness, it appears, was mirrored in the way the three actors performed on the stage. Individually, each of them was a perfectionist, so in combination . . . On the afternoon of the last day of the Broadway run Lynn approached Noël triumphantly with the news that she had finally devised a particular bit of business that had long eluded her. Yes, yes, she knew it was the closing night but at least she'd get to do it once!

This one communal acting experience inspired another Coward sketch . . .

DESIGN FOR REHEARSING

The scene is a bare stage with a few chairs and benches dotted about and a prompt table with a script, cigarettes, and chewing gum. Alfred and Lynn are discovered sitting up-stage opposite each other mumbling indistinctly. Noël enters in hat and coat.

NOËL: Hello, my little dears. I thought I was early.

ALFRED: We hadn't anything else to do so we got here at 10:15.

LYNN: Darling, I had a marvellous idea.

NOËL: (*Taking off hat and coat*) What?

LYNN: I'm not going to say "strawberry jam" like I did yesterday at all.

NOËL: How are you going to say it?

LYNN: Like this: "Strawberry Jam".

NOËL: Lovely. What scene shall we start with?

LYNN: You see, it's such an obvious change of mood there that it's better not to mark it too much, so if I tack "strawberry jam" on to the rest of it and then say it quite casually like this: "strawberry jam".

NOËL: Ever so much better.

LYNN: I'll do it the old way if you want me to but I did feel . . .

NOËL: Try it anyhow.

LYNN: You see, I think *she* would. You be Alfred for a moment and I'll show you what I mean. (*She grips his wrists*) "strawberry jam". There!

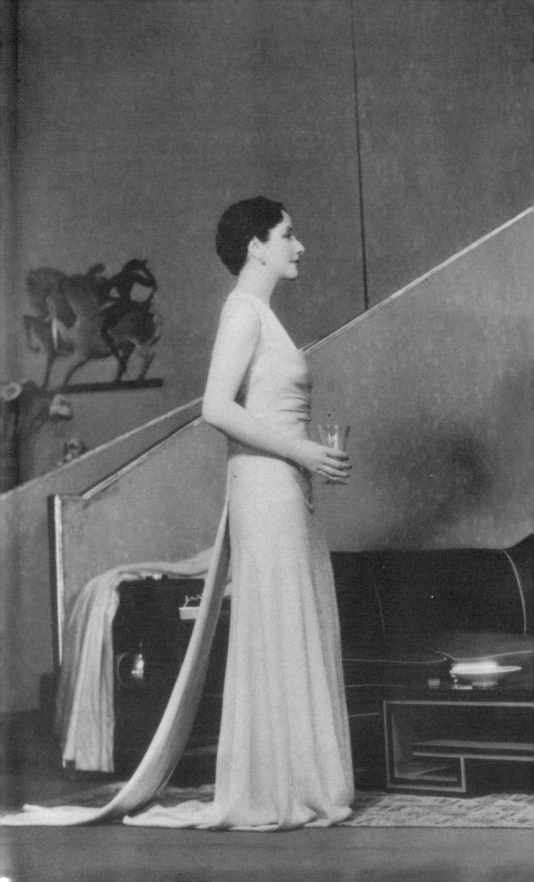

NOËL:	That's quite, quite magnificent, dear. Now what are we going to start with—you and Alfred in the second act?
ALFRED:	Oh, God, I was so *awful* in that scene yesterday—just an old stodgy Scandinavian Pudding.
NOËL:	I thought you were so excellent.
ALFRED:	No. No. No. I was awful—dreadful. I didn't sleep a wink all night—tossing about and turning I was, and pacing the floor.
LYNN:	Do you know what he did to me at 4:30 this morning?
NOËL:	I tremble to think.
LYNN:	His whole First Act and then we cooked some eggs
ALFRED:	I loathe my face, you know—it's horrible—no bone structure. I'd like to have a face like yours.
LYNN:	He's always wanted to have a face like yours.
NOËL:	Let's do your scene in the Second Act with Alfred.
LYNN:	No, darling. We can do that at home. Let's do one of your scenes.
NOËL:	All right. I'd like to say one thing, Alfred, before we begin. You're raving to say you were bad in that scene yesterday—it was perfectly enchanting, all through.
ALFRED:	(*Wailing*) Oh, no. No. No. No. It was terrible.
LYNN:	I was a shell, an empty shell, that's all I was, and I had a stomach ache.—You wait until I get my words slick.
ALFRED:	Do you know, Noel, this is the most *extraordinary* play! It's got a sort of—you know—an underneath—quality. It's fascinating—when I first read the script I got the most extraordinary feeling of *satisfaction*—like when I read *Karl and Anna*.
LYNN:	Never mind that now, darling. We must begin.
NOËL:	My entrance?
LYNN:	Yes.
ALFRED:	By the way, Noël, you did the most superb bit of business with the lid of the cigarette box yesterday. Don't change it—for God's sake don't change it!
NOËL:	Well, I wasn't quite sure—I thought it might be a little overdone.

ALFRED: No. No. No. It was enchanting. Larry noticed it—He said it was perfect.

LYNN: Larry does the most marvellous imitation of you. He did it last night in Alfred's hat.

ALFRED: I suppose you know this is the best play you've ever written.

LYNN: Do you realise we've never in our lives had a complete script to work on. We're quite dazed—we really are—dazed.

ALFRED: You remember, *Caprice*?

LYNN: Oh, my God!

NOËL: Come on, my entrance.

LYNN: (*Kissing him*) Darling, you won't be disheartened about yesterday, will you? It was the first time I'd touched the last Act without my book.

ALFRED: And don't worry about her making her entrance through the fire-place. The old girl has no bump of locality at all. She's walked through fire-places for years—Just the Santa Claus of Fifty-second Street.

NOËL: Let's not start with my entrance. We're very slick there. It's the end of the act that's so ragged.

ALFRED: That's my fault—I'm awful.

NOËL: No, it isn't—it's mine.

LYNN: I'll be all right when I get my words slick. God knows I realise I'm slow, but I've never been as slow as this. We're tired, you know—all those years learning part after part.

NOËL: Alfred's entrance.

ALFRED: All right

(*They take their places. Lynn and Noël laugh hysterically—Alfred enters.*)

ALFRED: Hallo, Leo

NOËL: Hallo, Otto.

ALFRED: Why did you stop laughing so suddenly?

NOËL: It's funny how lovely it is to see you.

ALFRED: Why funny?

(*Pause*)

NOËL: Come on, Lynn.

LYNN: Oh, God! let's go back. I shall always forget that line—always—always—always.

(They go back)

ALFRED: Hallo, Leo.

NOËL: Hallo, Otto.

ALFRED: Why did you stop laughing so suddenly?

NOËL: It's funny how lovely it is to see you.

ALFRED: Why funny?

(Pause)

LYNN: It's no use looking at me like that. I can't do anything if you look at me like that.

ALFRED: I wasn't looking at you at all.

LYNN: Oh yes, you were—you had a sneer on your face.

ALFRED: She always picks on me when she forgets her lines.

LYNN: I was word perfect in this scene last night and now Alfred's put me off entirely.

ALFRED: Nonsense.

LYNN: No. No. It's no good. When you're in this mood I can't act with you. It's not fun.

NOËL: Will you both of you shut up and get on with it?

LYNN: We're always like this, darling. You mustn't be disheartened. What's my line?

NOËL: "Where's Ernest?"

LYNN: Where's Ernest?

            Etc., Etc., Etc., until:

ALFRED: Oh, did you?

NOËL: Yes I did.

ALFRED: I see.

(Pause)

LYNN &
NOËL   *(Together)*: If only you wouldn't look like that.

LYNN: I shall never remember that line—never—never—never—

NOËL: I'll say it, then.

LYNN: No, I'll say it.

NOËL: All right—say it.

LYNN: Give it to me.

ALFRED: I see.

LYNN: If only you wouldn't look like that. You sat down there yesterday, Alfred.

ALFRED: Well, I'm standing up today.

LYNN: That's what's putting me off.

ALFRED: I don't see that it matters very much how I look.

           Etc., Etc., Etc., until:

LYNN: . . . It's overbalancing and disrupting everything.

NOËL: 'Distorting'.

LYNN: It's disrupting my part.

NOËL: I bet it isn't.

LYNN: I'll show you. Where's my bag.

                    (*They look for it*)

LYNN: Here. (*She produces part.*)

NOËL: (*Finding place*) There you are—'distorting'.

LYNN: Funny, I could have sworn it was disrupting.

NOËL: Never mind.

ALFRED: I *knew* it was distorting.

LYNN: Why didn't you say so?

ALFRED: Because you've already snapped my head off once this morning.

LYNN: It's silly to say things like that just because you're nervous about going to the dentist at four-thirty.

ALFRED: It's nothing to do with the dentist.

LYNN: Oh, yes it is (*to Noël*) It upsets him, you know

ALFRED: I think you must be sickening for something. You haven't behaved like this since *Strange Interlude.*

LYNN: Now, Alfred.

ALFRED: So disagreeable and snappy.

NOËL: (*Shouting them down*) Listen, both of you—listen -

LYNN:	What?
NOËL:	I shall never be able to play this part -
ALFRED:	Don't be so silly.
LYNN:	It's our fault—we're worrying him.
NOËL:	No. It's nothing to do with you—it's me—I'm wrong—I haven't got the feel of it—when I watch you—you're so meticulous, so superb it takes the ground from under my feet.
ALFRED & LYNN:	No. No. No.
NOËL:	Yes. Yes. Let's get somebody else and I'll just direct. Honestly—I'm so wretched—I shall never -
ALFRED:	You're wonderful. You're going to be better than you've *ever been in your life*.
LYNN:	You're so fluid and assured—you're a actor.
NOËL:	No. No. No.
ALFRED:	Yes. Yes. Yes. I'm the one who's going to let the play down.
NOËL:	No. No. No.
LYNN:	No. No. No.
ALFRED:	Yes. Yes. Yes. I'm awful.
LYNN:	No, darling, no. It's me not knowing my lines.
NOËL:	What does it matter about the lines?
ALFRED:	Let's go back and start all over again.
LYNN:	Yes. From the very beginning.
NOËL:	Don't you think we'd better start from my entrance.
LYNN:	Yes, darling—your entrance.
ALFRED:	It's my entrance that it gets so ragged.
NOËL:	All right.
ALFRED:	Hallo, Leo.
NOËL:	Hallo, Otto.
ALFRED:	Why did you stop laughing so suddenly?
NOËL:	It's funny how lovely it is to see you.
ALFRED:	Why funny?

Pause

ALFRED: Come on, Lynn

LYNN: *(Absently)* Where's Ernest?—I was wrong about that reading in the Second Act—it ought to be like this: Listen— "Strawberry jam"!

CURTAIN

(c.1933)

*   *   *   *

Noël took one further opportunity to tease his friends. In the original script for Operette *(1937)—a sort of Chekhovian* Hay Fever *set at a house party in Austria—two of the minor characters are Ruth Vernon and Latymer Chard (a thinly disguised Lynn and Alfred)—an acting duo who do nothing but rehearse their latest play. As a result, the* non sequitur *nature of their dialogue often confuses their fellow guests . . .*

There is the sound of raised angry voices in the distance and RUTH *and* LATYMER *come on from the direction of the lake)*

RUTH: How dare you—how dare you say such cruel things to me!

LATYMER: Because I once loved you and now I hate you—coldly and clearly I hate you . . .

RUTH: Go away—go away—

LATYMER: You belong to a race apart from me—it was sadness to imagine that we could ever be happy—you breathe different air—you see different suns, different moons, different stars—you're as alien to me as the East is alien to the West—you're . . .

RUTH: *(Wildly, crying)* Go away—go away—someone will hear . . .

LATYMER: I would wish the whole world to hear what I have to say to you—you have no power over me any more, do you understand that?—I'm free at last—Don't be afraid I shall not remember you—I shall always remember you, but not as I believed you to be, only as you are—empty and vain—a courtesan without conviction—a harlot without warmth!

RUTH: *(Striking him in the face)* You fool!

LATYMER: That wasn't right—do it lower down.

RUTH: Give it to me again.

LATYMER: . . . empty and vain—a courtesan without conviction, a harlot without warmth!

RUTH: *(Striking him again)* You fool!

(They go into the house)

*   *   *   *

*A star who spanned virtually the whole of Noël's own career was Beatrice
Lillie.*

*He saw her emerge as a comedienne during the first World War and
become a star of 1920s revue. In* Charlot's Revue of 1926—*in which she
performed some of Noël's own material—she received star billing over both
Gertie and Jack Buchanan.*

*In 1928 she co-starred with him in the Broadway production of his
own revue,* This Year of Grace *and three years later—in* The Third
Little Show—*it was Beattie (as he always called her) who introduced his
most famous song, "Mad Dogs and Englishmen".*

In 1938 he was to devise a whole revue (Set to Music) *around her
eccentric talents and it was in that show that she sang another famous
Coward 'first'—"Marvellous Party".*

*Like many of the talented people he was to work with, she was not
always an easy colleague. It was around this time that he wrote of her—"I
should like to say that she was then, and is now, a much-loved friend. The
fact that she was an uppish, temperamental, tiresome, disagreeable, incon-
siderate, insufferable friend during that one week of her life in no way sul-
lies my steadfast love for her. It may have temporarily dimmed it to the
extent of my wishing ardently to wring her neck, but once it had opened in
New York all rancour disappeared as the mist on a glass disappears with
the application of a damp rag . . .*

*"If I loathed her with every quivering fibre of my being, which at cer-
tain dress rehearsals I have done, I still have to admit that a visit with Bea
Lillie is one of the most enchanting things that could happen to anyone."*

*Twenty-five years later they were reunited one last time when the lady
played Madame Arcati in* High Spirits, *the musical version of* Blithe
Spirit—*which Noël had not written but was to direct. He was asked to
contribute a profile on "the funniest woman in the world" and was happy
to oblige . . .*

BEATRICE LILLIE–
AN APPRECIATION

The explanation of the word 'unique' in *Chamber's Twentieth Century Dictionary* is as follows—"Single or alone in any quality; without a like or equal". This word, in my opinion, applies to Beatrice Lillie more than to any other star in the world, with the possible exception of Charlie Chaplin. She is supremely single and alone and most certainly without a like or equal.

When she first comes onto the stage she imposes herself immediately and effortlessly on the audience. Her manner is a mixture of assurance and humility; she smiles not tentatively but hopefully, and suddenly, in a split second, she is loved, not merely laughed at or respected or admired, but loved. From that moment on whatever disasters, embarrassments, grotesqueries may bedevil her in the course of the performance, the sympathy and affection of the public is firmly ranged on her side. She may stray widely from the written script; she may interpolate on the spur of the moment words and phrases of her own which are far removed from the author's original intention and, as often as not, entirely irrelevant but the instinctive accuracy of her touch and her impeccable taste sweeps the by now hysterical audience into transports of laughter.

For an author, if he is wise, and not too obsessed with the sanctity of his own words, will stay resigned in his seat and laugh. If not he will fly out into the lobby and beat his head against the wall. In my own case, when faced with the erratic fantasies of Beatrice Lillie, I have found the former less agitating and the more sensible.

For an author or director to attempt to pin Beatrice down to a meticulous delineation of character is a direct invitation to nervous collapse. It isn't that she is unwilling or too sure of herself to take the trouble to learn "written" lines accurately. On the contrary, she tries with every fibre of her being to memorise every word. For the last many months and all through the rehearsal and try-out period for *High Spirits* she could be observed on the side of the stage or in her dressing room with her spectacles on her nose and her eyes glued to the script. Indeed, I am convinced that, even as I write these words, she is struggling away somewhere or other.

Deep down in her subconscious there is and always has been a sort of mental block about memorising lines accurately. As far back as 1928, when we were appearing together in *This Year of Grace*, I remember having a blazing row with her because she was singing my lyrics the wrong way round. In the forty-seven years that I have known her we have had three or four violent quarrels, none of which endured for more than twelve hours. During this recent production of *High Spirits* we have had none at all, with the exception of one black moment in New Haven, when she was under the impression that I had cut a scene which I hadn't cut and flew at me in no uncertain terms. Within an hour, however, she telephoned me at the hotel, admitted that she had completely misunderstood the situation and apologised with loving grace.

I have never encountered a star yet, including myself, who could not be a fiend when nervous and overwrought with pre-opening night tensions but I have known very few who were capable in so short a time of admitting they were wrong with such beguiling sincerity.

Beatrice Lillie has frequently been described by enthusiastic critics as 'the funniest woman in the world'. We have, of course, no absolute proof that that statement is correct. There may be, for all we and the critics know, Dyak matrons in the forests of Borneo, hilarious female pygmies lurking in the jungles of the Amazon or jolly veiled priestesses in some far flung spots to challenge the verdict that she is, in fact, the funniest woman of our time and our civilisation.

When I first met her in the latter part of World War 1, she was not, on the stage, funny at all. She was appearing in a revue at the Alhambra Theatre in London as a male impersonator. She was young, slim and as shiningly groomed as she is today. Her silk hat, white tie and tails were impeccable and she sang, irrelevant even at that early age, "I Want to Go Back to Michigan". The picture of that elegantly attired dandy yearning to return to a middle Western farm struck me, young as I was, as fairly incongruous.

Later, in the summer of 1917 when I, a reluctant recruit to the Armed Forces, was incarcerated in the First London General Military Hospital, I remember climbing over a gap in the wall one morning, rushing home and changing from my hospital 'blues' to a civilian suit and going to an opening matinee performance of an André Charlot revue called *Cheep!* at the Vaudeville Theatre. That performance turned out to be, in the light of later events, an historic occasion because it was the first time the sleek and urbane Beatrice Lillie appeared in her true colours as a comic genius of the first order.

In the first part of the revue she appeared as usual in her immaculate tails and sang, if I remember rightly, a song written specially for her by her sister Muriel, called "Take Me Back to the Land of Promise". The lyric, inspired by Muriel's obviously deep-seated fascination, dealt nostalgically with the blessings of being born a Canadian. The refrain ran as follows:

> *Oh, take me back to the la-and of Promise,*
> *Back to the land of the ice and the snows,*
> *There you and I together will wander*
> *Down lover's lane where the maple leaf grows.*
> *Skating—baseball and canoeing,*
> *That's the place to do your billing and cooing,*
> *Oh, take me back to the land I love be-est,*
> *Back to my little grey home in the west.*

When I explain that Beattie sang this with charm and sincerity and without the slightest humorous implication, the startling metamorphosis she achieved in the second act will be clearly understood. This metamorphosis occurred in a burlesque musical act called 'The Dedleighdul Quartette'. I forget the names of the other three performers but Miss Lillie, with high piled auburn hair, and a green satin evening gown from the bosom of which protruded a long stemmed chrysanthemum, will stay in my memory for ever. She sang, in a piercing soprano, a straight popular ballad called "Bird of Love Divine". She sang this also with apparently the utmost sincerity, but it did just occur to her during the second verse to prop her music up against the chrysanthemum. I believe I was still laughing when, a couple of hours later, I clambered back over the hospital wall in order to be discovered demurely in bed for evening roll call.

In the fairly long interim between 1918 and 1964 Beattie has sung many of my songs and played many of my sketches. I have appeared frequently with her not only on the professional stage in *This Year of Grace* but at countless charity performances and troop entertainments during World War II. On one occasion many years ago I actually joined her, at her own request, on her opening night in cabaret at the Rainbow Room, where we proceeded to sing, unrehearsed, with almost total inaccuracy, two duets which we had performed in the past.

I have directed her on three different occasions. *This Year of Grace* 1928, *Set To Music* 1938 and now *High Spirits* in 1964. I have known her gay and sad, bad tempered, good tempered, sober as a judge and high as a kite, but I have never known her do anything consciously vulgar or deliberately unkind.

And what, in this particular analysis, is perhaps most important of all, I have very very seldom known her fail to conquer and hold the public. Perhaps only two or three times I have seen an audience die on her. The reason for this being because she either stayed on too long or was insecure in her material. But those occasions have been very very rare.

I stated blithely a paragraph or two back that I directed her in three shows. This actually is a mis-statement. I have never really directed Beatrice Lillie any more than anyone else has. I have guided her, argued with her and, on occasion, squabbled with her but direction *qua* direction in her case is an academic term. She is not in the least non-cooperative. She listens attentively when told when to move and where to move and how to end a certain line and tries willingly and earnestly to comply, but the results are short-lived. Her instincts and her talent take command and her instinctive obedience to them is absolute. Her timing, contrary to what many critics have affirmed, is by no means always faultless. She is frequently guilty of ruining a comedy line by imposing on it a visually comic gesture. This is largely because her inventiveness is always moving ahead of what she is actually doing or saying.

She has little or no knowledge of 'acting' in the technical sense. Her experience in 'legitimate' comedy is naturally limited because she has only appeared in straight plays three or four times in her life. The trained give and take of a number of experienced actors playing a concerted scene is foreign to her. She establishes little or no contact with her fellow players on the stage, not from any delusions of superiority or conceit, but because it seldom occurs to her to look at them. She is the product of a different and, in many ways, a much harder school. Her own personal genius and experience have trained her to establish immediate contact with the audience. This, obviously enough, can be achieved much more easily when she is alone on the stage and has nobody else near her to deflect her primary and instinctive intention.

With one other person only she has no problems, providing always that she likes and respects that one other person enough to relax. On the various occasions I have appeared with her, I have found her completely unselfish and great fun to work with. But with more than one other person and with perhaps a complicated scene to play, she is subconsciously ill at ease.

However, the sum total of all this meticulous analysis becomes automatically null and void when she can still, after a long and triumphant career, walk on to a stage and completely subjugate hundreds of people eight times a week. Star quality is and always has been indefinable. In

Beattie's case it is authentic and valid and allied to a disciplined professionalism which is wholly admirable and completely reliable. I have never known her be late for a rehearsal. I have never actually known her to miss a performance and I can only say that, if she ever has, it must have been for a very good reason. She belongs to a great and rare theatrical vintage which is fast running out. Nor for her the easy and prevalent self-indulgences of hypochondria. Not for her the sudden onslaught of nervous exhaustion brought on by bad temper and being spoilt and too newly successful. When you read the name 'Beatrice Lillie' over a theatre marquee, you can be fairly certain, even if you have had to book your seat months ahead, that she will be there. And she will make her first entrance (unbeknownst to you, nervous as a kitten) and you will be aware, either consciously or unconsciously, that you are in the presence of a gallant, shining and indestructible star.

(1964)

*　　　　　*　　　　　*　　　　　*

*Bea Lillie happened to be a friend and she and Noël went back a long way.
But over those years he was to encounter a lot of talented artistes who tired
his patience . . .*

*"God preserve me . . . from female stars," he wrote in his Diaries. "I
don't suppose He will."*

Nor was the problem confined to female *stars. From the beginning of
his career he was witness to the impenetrable ego of the male matinée idol
and lampooned it early and often . . .*

THE ONE MAN PLAY

The scene is the office of Ritz Berkeley, a matinée idol.

RITZ: (*At telephone*) No, of course not . . . very well, old man . . .
yes, old man . . . no, old man . . . I won't play it . . . not my
type . . . dine at seven, is that all right? What did I think of
the show on Saturday? Terrible, old man . . . I'll let you
know . . . yes, I've got an author . . . young, brains, enthusiasm . . . thinks I'm the best actor in England . . . damn clever
. . . good bye.

                CHLOË *is stamping books at desk*

    What are you doing, Chloë?

CHLOË: Stamping all these autograph books with your signature.

RITZ: Well, do it outside and show Mr. Griggs up when he arrives.

CHLOË: Don't be cross, Ritzie dear—just 'cos it's Monday morning

                      (*Exits*)

RITZ: Damn everybody (*Snatches up phone*) Hullo, hullo, is that
you, Bertram? . . . Get me Sir Alfred Butt . . .(*Hangs up
receiver. Waits. Bell rings*) That you, Butt? . . . yes . . .*what*
matinée? No, Butt . . . Yes, Butt . . . Never, never, never . . .
Look here, Butt, it must be something with weight . . . give
and take, you know . . . very well, I won't play it . . . Elsie
Janis? No . . . No . . . Delysia? No, no, no . . . I want artists,
old man, artists! (*He rings off*) The man's a total fool!

                Enter CHLOË

CHLOË: Mr. Griggs to see you.

RITZ:	Didn't I tell you to show him up?
CHLOË:	All right, Ritzie darling—don't be fractious. (*Exits*)
RITZ:	Damn everything. (*At phone*) Get me Charlot. I'll hold on (*Pause*) That you, Charlot? . . . Yes, old man . . . about that play you sent me—terrible.

Enter NORMAN GRIGGS, *a Dramatist*

	Sit down, old man . . . yes . . . no . . . Fay Compton? God forbid . . . Constance Collier? Not on your life . . . Irene Vanbrugh? Fearful, old boy, fearful . . . I won't play with 'em (*Rings off*) Well?
GRIGGS:	You told me to come and see you—about my play!
RITZ:	So I should think—you ought to be downright ashamed of yourself . . .
GRIGGS:	Why?
RITZ:	It's awful, old man, awful!
GRIGGS:	Oh!
RITZ:	Where's your construction?
GRIGGS:	I don't know.
RITZ:	Where's your dialogue?
GRIGGS:	(*Pointing to play on desk*) There.
RITZ:	Don't be silly, old boy. Understand once and for all—this play of yours is hopeless—dreadful.
GRIGGS:	May I have it back, then?
RITZ:	What the hell for?
GRIGGS:	To send to someone else.
RITZ:	Try not to be a fool, old man. Try not to be a fool. I'm going to do it all right.
GRIGGS:	(*Brightening*) I thought you said it was hopeless?
RITZ:	So it is. We must work on it together.
GRIGGS:	It's complete as it is.
RITZ:	Complete, my foot. (*Telephone rings*) Hello, hello . . . look here, what the hell did you send me that script for? You know I can't read German. What, old man? Moscovitch? Never . . . Leslie Henson. Good God, no . . . Phyllis

	Monkman—don't be funny (*He rings off*) Now about this play of yours . . .
GRIGGS:	(*Hesitant*) Yes?
RITZ:	Who have you got in your mind's eye for the leading lady?
GRIGGS:	(*Timidly*) Madge Titheradge.
RITZ:	Hopeless, old man. No depth.
GRIGGS:	Iris Hoey.
RITZ:	Worse. No breadth.
GRIGGS:	Gladys Cooper?
RITZ:	Look here, old boy—I'm serious, you know—what about Lucy Wittlebot?
GRIGGS:	Who's Lucy Wittlebot?
RITZ:	You mean you haven't seen me dancing with her at The Embassy?
GRIGGS:	Oh yes, I remember now.
RITZ:	That girl's got talent. She's never had a chance yet.
GRIGGS:	Is she quite the type?
RITZ:	Type be damned. She's young, fresh, pretty. What more do you want!
GRIGGS:	Oh, all right.
RITZ:	And see here—you've got to build up that part for me. I can't play it as it is.
GRIGGS:	Build it up? But . . .
RITZ:	What do you think I put on plays for—to see other people act in 'em? You're a young author and you've got to learn the *right* way to do things. I'm going to *mould* you. Now then, for instance, in this script you allow me to be discovered on the stage when the curtain goes up.
GRIGGS:	Well, why not?
RITZ:	Try to be intelligent. Why *not*! I'm your star—I'm the crux of your show. I must have an entrance down a staircase.
GRIGGS:	(*In anguish*) But it's a river bungalow. You can't have staircases in a river bungalow.

RITZ: Don't argue, old boy, don't argue. I'm telling you how to make your play a success.

GRIGGS: Oh!

RITZ: Then you must give me a good comedy scene when I hide under the bed.

GRIGGS: But why should you hide under the bed in your own home?

RITZ: Ingenuous youth! I hide under the bed because I know her husband is outside.

GRIGGS: But she's unmarried?

RITZ: Don't be silly, old man—give her a husband.

GRIGGS: But . . . but . . .

RITZ: That's it . . . but-but-but-but-but! Can't you see I'm trying to help you? You've got to give me a lovely little scene when I stand in the window with the moonlight all round me. Then you must work it somehow so that I have a big scuffle with two armed men. Then you must give me the final curtain with the room in darkness and me sitting gazing into the fire and saying—"I wonder".

GRIGGS: You seem to have forgotten that this is a simple psychological comedy.

RITZ: Simple psychological poppycock. What you want is a commercial success (*To himself*) I don't know what's happened to the theatre today. I might as well write the damn thing myself.

GRIGGS: (*Gulping*) Oh!

BLACKOUT

(1921)

Did someone say—"Shades of Garry Essendine"?

CHAPTER FOUR

TOGETHER WITH MUSIC

Together with music,
Together with music . . .
And shadows seem to fade away.
Many a vanished moon and June
Enchant us again,
Many a long forgotten tune
Brings back its old refrain.

"Together with Music"
Duet with Mary Martin
From 1955 TV special

THROUGHOUT HIS CAREER NOËL NEVER VENTURED FAR FROM THE MUSICAL theatre that had been such a formative influence on him in the early part of the century. Years later he reflected on the form . . .

MUSICAL COMEDY

On my fifth birthday my mother injected the 'Musical Comedy' virus into my bloodstream by taking me to see *The Dairymaids* at the Grand Theatre, Croydon. All I can clearly remember of it is the opening chorus in an elaborate dairy where a number of young ladies were skittishly manipulating butter churns and the opening chorus of the second act when, confusingly, the same young ladies were vaulting about in a gymnasium in a high school and executing a complicated dance routine with indian clubs. Delighted but bewildered by all this, I questioned my mother closely but her explanations were vague and unsatisfactory. However, it established in my mind the conviction that 'Musical Comedy' was gaily irrational to the point of lunacy, a conviction I have strongly upheld for over sixty years. My mother was what would be christened in today's American slang a genuine Musical Comedy Buff.

This is easily accounted for by the fact that during her long married years she appeared humbly but repeatedly in the chorus of the Teddington Amateur Dramatic Society's productions of Gilbert and Sullivan. When she took me to the theatre for birthday and other treats it was always to a musical comedy. In fact, I never saw a 'straight' play until I was eleven and had been on the stage professionally for a year.

This first 'straight' play I saw was a comedy called *Better Not Enquire*, starring Charles Hawtrey at the Prince of Wales Theatre. No prescient inner voice whispered to me that within six months I should be acting at that same theatre with Hawtrey himself in a play called *The Great Name* in which I had one line, as a page boy, in the last act.

In those early years my favourite musical comedy actress was Miss Gracie Leigh, who always played second (soubrette) parts. In the window of Keith Prowse I saw a playbill advertising *The Quaker Girl* on which she headed the female cast list. There was another playbill overlapping this and so it was not until mother and I had forced our way into the front row of the pit and opened our programmes that we noticed the four magic words "And Miss Gertie Millar". Presently she made her entrance with all the Quakers, detached herself from them, glided across the stage to Joseph Coyne, who was sitting under a tree, and proceeded to sing and dance their first duet, "When A Good Girl Like Me Meets A Bad Boy Like You". From that moment onward I was enslaved.

Many years later I went with her to the opening night of a revival of *The Quaker Girl*, which was less than elegantly performed, and I remember her putting her hand gently on my knee to restrain my irritated twitchings and quell my emotional imprecations. To me Gertie Millar was and is—now, alas, only in my memory—the epitome of what a musical comedy star should be, as indeed *The Quaker Girl* was the epitome of what a musical comedy should be. It had a good story, excellent lyrics and, above all, an exciting score by Lionel Monckton. Embedded in my mind for ever is the vision of Gertie Millar singing in the moonlit garden of the Pre-Catalan, moving with such feather-light grace that she seemed to be floating rather than dancing.

In the days of my youth Musical Comedy stars were a good deal more insouciant in regard to their work and their public than they are today. They 'stayed off' on the slightest pretext. I remember waiting for hours in pit and gallery queues to see Lily Elsie in *The Merry Widow*, *The Dollar Princess* and *The Count of Luxembourg* but I never actually caught up with her until she played *Paula* at the Palace theatre in the mid-Twenties. She was, of course, enchanting but I cannot resist sending an affectionate 'Thank you' back over the years to Miss Deborah Volar, her understudy, whom I saw so often and knew so much better. I was much luckier with my adored Gertie Millar, on one occasion miraculously so. I opened my programme and there was the sinister little slip announcing that "owing to indisposition, etc., Miss Millar's part would be played by Miss Whoever-It-Was." I seethed with disappointment and contemplated for a moment leaving the theatre and going to a movie but, as I was being taken as a special treat by an old friend who had booked the seats (dress circle front row) weeks before, I crushed down my gloom and determined to enjoy the show for what it was worth. It was fortunate that I did because on she came, my beloved star, as magical as ever. Of course the age old tradition that a star must appear even if he or she are practically dying is an excellent one, although it can be carried too far. I once played a performance of *The Knight of the Burning Pestle* with a temperature of 103° and gave sixteen members of the company mumps, thereby closing the play and throwing everybody out of work. There may be a moral lurking somewhere in this but I cannot for the life of me discern what it is.

Musical Comedy was, I believe, originally devised by the late George Edwardes as a happy compromise between the continental operettas of Lecoq and Offenbach, the early Burlesques of the old Gaiety Theatre and the hearty, clean-limbed but melodious high jinks of Gilbert and Sullivan. In my youth nearly all musical comedies had "Girl" titles: *The Girl From Cook's, The Girl in the Taxi, The Girl in the Film, The Sunshine Girl, The Girl From Utah, The Girl in the Train,* etc. Every now and then a 'Maid' or two edged their way onto the playbill: *The Spring Maid, The Rebel Maid, The Maid of the Mountains* but on the whole the 'Girls' won hands down. In most of these entertainments there was nearly always a bitter misunderstanding between the hero and the heroine at the end of the first act (if it was a two acter) or the second (if it was in three acts). Either he would insult her publicly or, discovering that she was a Princess in her own right instead of the simple commoner he had imagined her to be or she would wrench her engagement ring from her finger and fling it at his feet and faint dead away or, realising that he was not the humble tutor she had loved for himself alone but a multi-millionaire. The ultimate reconciliation was usually achieved a few seconds before the final curtain after the leading comedian had sung a topical song and there was nothing left to do but forgive and forget.

The Musical Comedies of today are less encumbered with social overtones; the problems of disguised Princes and Princesses have given way to the more realistic machinations of spies and crooks and gangsters, who provide more excitement perhaps but, for me, less nostalgia. I still miss the anguished second act finale misunderstanding between the hero and the heroine and I still long to hear the leading lady cry with a breaking heart—"Play louder—play louder—I want to dance and forget!" Personally, I have not the least desire for the music to play louder—I certainly do not want to dance and forget. What I do want, however, and fully intend to do, is to look back over the years and with a grateful smile, remember."

(1969)

*   *   *   *

*Noël was never to produce a musical comedy by that definition. For him the 1920s were devoted to the revue form—*London Calling! *(1923),* On With the Dance *(1925) and* This Year of Grace *(1928)—and his first 'book' musical,* Bitter Sweet *(1929) but it might so easily have been otherwise.*

Somewhere around 1923 he began a collaboration with Jerome Kern that appears to have gone unrecorded in either man's correspondence.

By this time Noël was beginning to visit the US regularly and Kern himself had been a regular transatlantic commuter since early in the century. Consequently, it would have been surprising if the two men had not met. Collaboration would also have been perfectly possible, since in the course of his career Kern was known to have collaborated with over seventy lyricists.

Spread over several notebooks are Noël's notes for the libretto and lyrics, together with his notes "To Mr. Kern" indicating the kind of song he had in mind by reference to earlier Kern numbers in the period up to 1923. Sheet music discovered in the famous Secaucus, New Jersey warehouse treasure trove of 1986 proves that Kern did, in fact, set music to two of them.

TAMARAN

The plot of the show, Tamaran, *was par for the period course. A young man comes to work in a fashion shop but he is, in reality, the exiled Crown Prince of the mythical impoverished European country,* Tamaran. *He falls in love with a young girl who works there, who, unbeknown to him, is also* Tamarani—*from which point the ending is inevitable. The store is owned by Atlas Blubb, a vulgar couturier. (The role was intended for Leslie Henson, the leading light comedian of the day, who specialised in* double entendre *and malapropisms).*

CHORUS LADY: Could I see you for a moment, Mr. Blubb?

ATLAS: What is it?

CHORUS LADY: It's about some dresses for Drury Lane next Monday. I shall want three altogether. The first one just a simple peasant dress—you know, sort of Swiss thing with white stockings and wooden shoes and long fair wig. Then I am Queen Elizabeth; of course, I should like something very special for that—and in the last part of the show I am Charlotte Corday. The Stage Manager said you'd know who she was.

ATLAS: Oh, certainly, very old family

CHORUS LADY: A French lady, I believe, who poisoned a gentleman in his bath.

ATLAS: Take this lady's measurements, Hadley. Will you want the dresses new or from stock?

CHORUS LADY: Oh, thank you, Mr. Blubb. Of course, I would like to have them all made for me, but there won't be much time before Monday.

ATLAS: Who do I send the account to?

CHORUS LADY: The account?

ATLAS: Yes, we have to live you know. Are you paying for them yourself?

CHORUS LADY: Oh no; they said you knew all about it—it's a benefit performance. It says in the papers "Costumes kindly lent by Atlas Blubb. *(She shows him paper which he snatches from her and reads)*

ATLAS: "Grand Matinée—Be Kind To The Parrot Fund". You will want a pair of No.2 hips for Queen Elizabeth, and if you haven't got a bath for the Charlotte Corday scene, come round to my house and I'll give you one.

Oh, go upstairs and help yourself.

(Enter young actor (WINTHROP) with Henry VIII doublet and trunks over his trousers with comic Irishman's wig with bald front, which doesn't fit. He is followed by HEREFORD)

WINTHROP: I call it a perfect disgrace;

HEREFORD: Well, they are the orders I had, and I must say I cannot see anything wrong with it, you had better speak to the boss.

(Noise of motor and horn heard. Three or four of the assistants return to their places. A motor is seen arriving through the shop window, and ATLAS BLUBB enters briskly. He is a dapper little man in correct town clothes but wearing a country hat and overcoat. He is slightly lady-like in his manner, but this is chiefly a pose, which he occasionally drops and becomes distinctly authoritative. Though meticulous in his speech, he has a difficulty with his h's.   He is followed into the shop by his chauffeur, a young man with fair curly hair and a ridiculous light blue livery.)

ATLAS;   Bring in them parcels Knatchbull; put them over there – anywhere you like; what's everybody doing? nothing of course. Anyone would think I run this place as an amusement park.

Knatchbull;   (in a very high voice) What about the basket of eggs?

ATLAS;   You can take them round to Lady Whichwhat's at her studio in Berkeley Mews, say "With Mr.Blubb's compliments, and I 'ope the Cleopatra dress was alright" and put in one of my almanacks.   I shall want the car round at half past six; I am going round to do the Duchess's hair (He commences to open letters)
What Her Grace would do without me I am sure I don't know. That maid of her's is a perfect fool . . . .
Well, what's doing?

Assistant;   Mr.Keys has been in Sir.

Atlas;   Bunch! What does he want?

Asst.   He didn't say Sir; said he wanted to see you personally;

Atlas;   I dare say he did; you can tell him I am not at the call of every Dick,Tom,and Harry that comes round bothering. Perhaps he would like me to stay with him for the week-end.
Anything else?

2nd Asst.   Yes Sir, Mr.Ainley......

Atlas;   Who's he?

2nd Asst;   Mr.Henry Ainley,Sir.

Atlas;   Oh; Ahesan.

2nd Asst;   His dresser 'phoned sir to say that his new beard is all wrong.

Atlas;   Well, tell him to grow one himself.
Take down this letter Miss Jenkins ;–

WINTHROP: Speak to the boss; I should say I will speak to the boss.

ATLAS: What is it? What is it? I can't have you walking about my establishment making complaints in a loud voice.

WINTHROP: I'll make something else if I don't get some attention; look at this costume.

ATLAS: Very handsome

WINTHROP: First big chance I get in all my career; dress rehearsal tonight, and look what you have sent me down.

ATLAS: Henry VIII

WINTHROP: Henry VIII? *(Pointing to his wig)* Do you call this Henry VIII?

ATLAS: *(Turning the wig around)* You have got it on the wrong way. That beard is all wrong, Hereford. The gentleman certainly has cause for complaint there; give me a scissors.

WINTHROP: Beard, be damned; I am not playing Henry VIII—it's Henry V.

ATLAS: Well, what does it matter whether it's 8th or 5th—if it isn't in the first three.

WINTHROP: You know I'll go somewhere else if you are not careful.

ATLAS: You'll go there anyhow whether I am careful or not

Meanwhile, the rebel government now in charge of Tamaran is advertising for a King—something which actually happened in Albania!—and Atlas decides to apply. His girl friend, Zaza, can already see herself as Queen . . .

ZAZA: I think you're wonderful—I know you will be a riot—

ATLAS: Riot! You bet I will—I can feel the spirit of Napoleon working in me now—

*(A native girl comes to the table with a tray of sweets—*ATLAS *motioning her away)*

Not tonight, Josephine! There, what did I tell you?

ZAZA: Where you'll succeed is that you have personality—you'll be an attractive king.

(She runs her hand lightly along the table—touching his, and withdraws it again)

ATLAS: Well, God knows I've had enough experiences—just look at the Royalties I've mixed with—in and out of the shop all day they are—underclothes with coronets on are no treat to me!

ZAZA: Your court will be a mass of Diplomatic Intrigue and *affaires du coeur*!

ATLAS: I shall hold me levees in bed in the morning—like Louis the Fourteenth.

ZAZA: (*Coyly*) I hope you'll have an attractive Queen.

ATLAS: I hadn't thought of that—

ZAZA: (*Firmly taking his hand*) I had—

ATLAS: Look 'ere, Zaza—I'll promise you something—When I get to Tamaran—

ZAZA: Shhhh—don't talk so loud—

ATLAS: I'll institute enquiries—you see in the advertisement it says "bachelors essential". (*He produces paper and shows it to her*)

ZAZA: What does that matter? If you're King, you can do anything.

ATLAS: 'Ow would you like to come and be my morganatic wife?

ZAZA: What's that?

ATLAS: Well—it's—er—it's rather more—er—rather less—

ZAZA: (*Rising*) How dare you—

ATLAS: Oh, keep calm—don't make a scene 'ere

ZAZA: You've insulted me, you miserable little beast—!

ATLAS: Well, Madame Pompadour and Dubarry didn't do so badly by being insulted—

ZAZA: (*Sitting down again*) Oh!

ATLAS: The authentic queens seem to me to 'ave 'ad a pretty poor time taken all round—

ZAZA: As a matter of fact, gay women are always much easier to play than straight ones—

ATLAS: I would build you a couple of palaces—and you would have two black pages to hold up your reputation!

ZAZA: When I think of the Publicity—

ATLAS: Publicity—you've said it—you'd be the most talked of

woman in the world—the Power behind the Throne—
You'd be able to 'old courts on your own—

ZAZA: Mary Pickford's face would be a study!

ATLAS: Mrs. Talmadge would have another daughter out of sheer pique!

ZAZA: It *does* sound wonderful. Tell me what morganatic means.

ATLAS: Well it's not in *Debrett*—but I've read about it somewhere!

MORGANATIC LOVE

ATLAS: Any king
May have his fling
But when it comes to love
A bitter sacrifice
He always has to make.

ZAZA: Royalties
Have loyalties
Which have to be considered
When the morale
Of the country is at stake.

ATLAS: I'd like to take you for my own
And plant you firmly on the throne
But, as I'm King
You'll understand
We'll have to be
More underhand . . .

BOH: We'll have a spree
Morganatically

ZAZA: For we agree
Love is free
Most emphatically.

ATLAS: We'll manage things
Diplomatically

ZAZA: And as we can't be good,
               We'll lead a careful life

ATLAS: If you will only be
               My morganatic wife.
               And we will lead them all
               The devil of a life
               When you're my cozy little
               Morganatic wife.

BOTH: And we will lead them all
               The devil of a life

ATLAS: When you're my
ZAZA: When I'm your

BOTH: Cozy little
               Morganatic wife!

(c.1923/4)

*   *   *   *

Why Coward and Kern never finished the piece remains unclear. Both were certainly busy and they went their separate ways to other and greater successes. But the answer may well be that each of them was coming to the conclusion that the musical comedy form had had its day. The young Noël (24)—with The Vortex *already on his mind—may have concluded that this kind of froth would no longer appeal to a beaded and beady mid-twenties audience.*

What is certain is that the two men remained the closest of friends to the end of Kern's life in 1945. In 1941 Noël dedicated a song to him, which incidentally sums up the fate of 'their' show. It was called "We Are Living in a Changing World". A year later Jerry Kern returned the compliment. Remembering Noël's love of a war-beleaguered Europe, he and Oscar Hammerstein dedicated their Academy Award-winning "The Last Time I Saw Paris" to their mutual friend.

*   *   *   *

Through the 1930s Noël's preferred musical form was the operetta—which he determinedly called operette.

1934's Conversation Piece *was "a romantic comedy with music", written specifically with the French star, Yvonne Printemps in mind. Of all his leading ladies she was perhaps his favourite, certainly for the quality of her singing.*

The evocatively-named Mlle. Printemps (1895-1977) was born with the more mundane name of Wignolle but her stage name suited her to perfection and she was one of the few artistes Noël was to regard with undimmed admiration and affection. She made her name in a series of Folies-Bergères revues in Paris between 1908 and 1915 and then extended her repertoire to include straight plays. In this she was greatly helped by the man whose second wife she became—Sacha Guitry, regarded by many as the 'French Noël Coward' because of his theatrical versatility. Guitry (1885-1957) was more inclined to think of Noël as the 'English Sacha Guitry', having established himself much earlier. He and Printemps were divorced in 1932 and Noël's friendship and allegiance remained with her. Guitry he came to consider "a pompous ass", a verdict perhaps conditioned by the suspicion that, along with many others in the French pre-war social-theatrical circle, Guitry had later collaborated with the Germans.

In 1934 he persuaded Yvonne—by now a major French star with a following in both London and New York—to come to London and star in his new operette, Conversation Piece. *The idea of writing a star vehicle for her had been C. B. Cochran's and was one Noël enthusiastically accepted. Because of the lady's tenuous grasp of English, he had to construct something that would not create undue strain for her. In a last minute casting change, he decided to play opposite her for a while, before relinquishing the part to her new husband-to-be, Pierre Fresnay. Some years later there was talk of her starring in a revival of the later* Operette, *a suggestion which led Noël to reflect on their relationship.*

YVONNE PRINTEMPS

"According to present day standards of biographical writing, I warn the reader here and now that this essay on Yvonne Printemps will be a disappointment. It should, I know, be witty, analytical and detached; it should, above all, be critical. Praise of her assets should be immediately qualified by sharp emphasis on her defects. It is no longer entertaining to members of the public to read that an artiste sings beautifully unless they are informed in the same paragraph that her diction is faulty and her acting leaves much to be desired; it also delights them to be told that although her phrasing of the aria in act three was quite perfect, she is too old for the part and her legs are too short.

We have in fact nowadays all been hypnotised by the newspapers of the world into believing that 'Bad news is Good news and Good news is No news'. Personally I do not subscribe to this arbitrary dictum. I am sick to death of bad news. I am weary of hearing artists and works of art belittled by mediocre minds; I prefer abuse to qualified praise and I have long ago given up any hope of finding anything constructive in professional criticism. The opinions of my fellow artists are all that interest me, because experience has taught me that they are the only ones who have enough knowledge of the *métier* to justify them.

Every now and then in our curious world of the theatre a unique star is born. They are rare, these gifted changelings and their uniqueness lies, not necessarily in their talent but in that particular quality they possess which defies comparison with anyone else; and it is of course, this indefinable quality that defeats criticism. Professional critics must have a yardstick with which to measure their values and the yardstick they use with monotonous regularity is comparison. Take this away from them and they are lost, befuddled and liable to make even greater asses of themselves than usual.

It is permissible, obviously, to prefer Eleanora Duse to Sarah Bernhardt, for instance, just as it is permissible to like an oak tree better than an elm tree but it is foolish to say that one is superior to the other. It should, therefore, be possible to discuss an individual artist without dragging in his or her contemporaries or predecessors. I am aware that Kirsten Flagstad sings better than Yvonne Printemps and that Anna Pavlova probably danced better than Tamara Karsivina but I should not care to see Pavlova in *La Tricorne*, Karsivina in *Le Mort du Cygne*, Flagstad in *Les Trois Valses* or Printemps in *The Ring*. In my forty years in the theatre I have known thousands and thousands of fine actors, actresses, singers and dancers but only a few who were great stars. Yvonne Printemps falls into the latter category not because she is in the least like any of them but because she is like none of them. All that she has in common with them is her uniqueness and the fact that her name is part of the structure of her world and the history of her time.

It is for me a difficult task to write a critical analysis of Yvonne Printemps in *Operette* for the simple reason that ever since I first beheld her in the first act of a play sitting up in bed and singing "J'ai deux

Monsieur Noël Coward
avec mon souvenir le
meilleur
Yvonne Printemps
1930

amants", she has completely disarmed my critical faculties. In the years following I have heard her in *Mozart, Mariette, Les Trois Valses* and my own operette, *Conversation Piece*, which I wrote and composed for her. I have heard her sing when she was so nervous that she could hardly stand. I have heard her sing when she was sad, gay and in every mood in between. But the occasion I will always remember was one occasion when we were lunching at her home. Her husband, Pierre Fresnay was present and the conversation was easy and relaxed. The food was more than perfect and there was a great deal of it. We had exquisite soup, *truite au bleu*, a *tête de veau*, salad and cheese and a chocolate *soufflé*. The sun was rather hot and so we retired indoors for coffee. Suddenly, with her coffee still unfinished, Yvonne, without rising from the sofa, sang the aria from *Madame Butterfly*, unaccompanied and full out. Her voice was pure and effortless and her breathing apparently non-existent. Pierre smiled indulgently and offered me some armagnac but I could neither refuse it nor accept it, because my eyes had filled with tears and I was speechless.

I am grateful to Yvonne Printemps for many such moments. There is something in her voice, not only her singing voice but her speaking voice, that pierces the heart immediately. Only last week when I was in Paris with Vivien Leigh and Laurence Olivier we went to see *Hymène*. The curtain rose and there was Yvonne, an invalid, seated in a wheel chair. She started to speak, quite ordinarily, quite simply, and the usual magic occurred, clearly and unmistakably. I glanced at Vivien and Larry next to me. Their eyes were shining and Vivien was fumbling silently in her bag for her handkerchief.

By now it must be fairly apparent to the reader that my considered opinion of Yvonne Printemps in *Operette* or out of it is favourable to say the least. But I really cannot allow my personal affection for her to blind me to her faults, one of which is her resolute determination not to sing a note on the stage unless she is forced to. In private life she will sing at the drop of a hat. I have heard her in a restaurant, happy and relaxed, open her mouth and warble like a bird but the thought of singing on the stage sends her into a pathological frenzy. It is a peculiar nervousness I have never encountered before and she is seized with it not only on opening nights, when it would be understandable, but on every other night as well. I have seen her over and over again in *Conversation Piece* waiting in the wings, clasping and unclasping her hands and shaking. There is no apparent reason for this: it is a sort of self-imposed masochism. It isn't that she has ever failed in a singing role; on the contrary, her public love for her to sing, her friends love for her to sing, even the critics love for her to sing. She has never, to my knowledge, had anything but triumphant success as a singer and I am sure that it is only the fact that she is such a fine actress that prevents people from going to the box office and demanding their money back when they have seen her in a straight play in which she doesn't sing one note.

In *Conversation Piece* she had, of course, one supreme reason to be nervous. She was playing and singing a long role in a foreign language. In latter years when I played one of my own plays (*Present Laughter—Joyeux Chagrins*) in Paris in French I understood only too well what she must have suffered. I at least could understand and speak French fairly fluently and still found it a terrible ordeal. She, on the other hand, knew no English at all and, I regret to say, however, that by the end of the run of *Conversation Piece* most of the English company spoke French excellently.

She arrived in London for the first rehearsal word perfect, having been working on the part phonetically for many weeks—but to little avail, as far as their meaning was concerned. I can still see her attacking those inimical English words with tremendous vehemence and then suddenly collapsing in fits of laughter.

The English company adored her from the first day but after two weeks of rehearsal they became a little puzzled by the fact that she never sang. Each day when the time came to do the number Yvonne would stand by the piano mouthing the words to herself but emitting no sound. One evening at the beginning of the third week I was directing the second half ballroom scene from my point of vantage in the front row of the dress circle. The theatre was empty except for a few understudies sitting in the stalls and my own immediate entourage, consisting of my secretary, Lorn Loraine, John C. Wilson, my manager and G. E. (Gladys) Calthrop, who had designed the production. The ballroom scene was difficult to direct because the whole cast was on the stage at the same time and I was beginning to get rather irritable. The moment came for Yvonne to sing her aria, "Plus de coeur discret" and, as usual, I expected her to stand quite still and mouth it soundlessly. The rehearsal accompanist struck the first introductory chords and suddenly, without warning, she decided to sing. The company who, up to that moment, had never heard her utter a vocal sound, stood transfixed. She sang the whole aria through passionately and divinely and the effect was electrifying. She finished with her arms outstretched and the last lovely B flat echoing though the empty theatre; there was a moment's stunned silence and the whole cast went mad. They shouted and cheered: Yvonne, of course, dissolved into floods of tears immediately. Personally, I was moved beyond words. It was a supreme "theatre" moment for theatre people. No layman living outside the walls of our enchanted citadel could have appreciated the true significance of it.

And in it, curiously enough, lay the essence of Yvonne Printemps. At a command performance she will sing beautifully to the kings and queens of the world. On an opening night she will sing superbly to ill mannered late-comers and cantankerous critics, but to her own people in a half lit, empty theatre she will sing with her whole heart and the heart of Yvonne Printemps is even greater than her talent."

*   *   *   *

His experience with Pacific 1860, *his first post-war musical ("a musical romance") was much less happy. After a great deal of rewriting and recasting, the part of the great diva, Madame Salvador finally went to Mary Martin.*

As he had found with Gertie and Bitter Sweet *and would again with Mary Ellis in* After the Ball *(1954), he had a leading lady who lacked the vocal range to sing the part he had written.*

Nonetheless, Mary was a genuine Broadway star, "a dream girl, quick and knowledgeable with all the mercurial charm of Gertie at her best with a sweet voice and more taste". Such was Noël's impression at the start of production. By the time the show opened in 1946 at the recently-repaired but still unheated Drury Lane ("Dreary Lane"), he suspected he had a disaster on his hands and Miss Martin's increasing tantrums—usually expressed through her husband, Richard Halliday—suggested she knew it, too.

With his impeccable show business training, Noël managed to keep his feelings largely to himself but he expressed them privately in a piece of verse he then tucked away in his files . . .

I RESENT YOUR ATTITUDE TO MARY

I resent your attitude to Mary.
It betrays a very ugly sort of mind.
She is innocent and pure
And her husband, I am sure,
Would consider your behaviour rather rude and *most*
    unkind.

Tho' his temperament is somewhat airy-fairy,
Which emerges when he's just a little blind.
He resents and I resent
And all the passers-by resent
Your hideous attitude to Mary.

I resent your attitude to Mary,
You only send her flowers once a day
Tho' her voice is apt to jar,
She's a *very* famous star
And she's only taking ten per cent for acting in your
    play.
Tho' her husband's heel is rather hairy,
He does very nicely on her pay.
He resents and she resents
And even Sylvia C. resents
Your beastly attitude to Mary

(1946)

A few years later all was forgiven, if not forgotten and they were again—
together with music.

*   *   *   *

IVOR NOVELLO

"The two most beautiful things in the world are Ivor's profile and my mind."

Noël first met Ivor Novello in 1917 when they were both appearing in Manchester in different plays. Despite the press insisting that there was a professional feud between them, they became immediate friends and friendly rivals.

In those early years they even wrote the occasional song together and Ivor played the lead in a Coward play, Sirocco *(1926)—which was a resounding flop!—and the film version of* The Vortex *(1927), which most certainly was not.*

But it was in the 1930s and 1940s that their musical careers began to run in parallel.

Noël tasted success first with the 1929 Bitter Sweet *and Ivor could not have been more generous in his appreciation of his achievement. In a letter he wrote:*

> "I've just come back from seeing *Bitter Sweet* for the second time and I've got to tell you what a *lovely, lovely* thing you have done— it's sheer joy from beginning to end. The music impressed me unbelievably—it's so gay yet full of thought and has the most extraordinary way of reflecting the story as it goes along. The only disconcerting thing about it is that I cry the moment the first note starts and *cannot* stop—the whole thing is so full of regret—not only for that darling lover who died but for a vanished kindly silly darling age you've re-created. I bless you for it and take off hat, drawers, nay sock suspenders to you for it . . . It's all so clear cut that one remembers the smallest detail. Your own mind is so un-blurred and you've used it like a painter's series of brushes, yet each stroke is so defining."

But from the day that Ivor—almost accidentally—wrote Glamorous Night *(1935), the show that single-handedly revived the fortunes of Drury Lane, he virtually owned the operetta form.*

Crest of the Wave *(1937),* The Dancing Years *(1939),* Perchance to Dream *(1945) and* King's Rhapsody *(1949) all played to packed houses of middle class matrons, yearning for romance. Admittedly, Noël had many more different irons in the fire than Ivor by this time but it always irked him that he was never able to repeat the success he had enjoyed with* Bitter Sweet *in this particular milieu.*

Sandy Wilson probably hit on the reason when he observed that "Noël's wit sprang from his intellect". He had a romantic streak, whereas Ivor was a true romantic. In his shows he wore his heart boldly on his sleeve—and his public adored him for it.

In 1951 Noël was asked to write the introduction for a biography of Ivor. He willingly did so but before the book could be published, Ivor, who was appearing in his own King's Rhapsody, *went home after a performance and died of a heart attack. Ruritania died with him. Noël asked for the preface to be withdrawn . . .*

"The name Ivor Novello is euphonious; it is pleasant to say, to hear and to see. It is also one of the most famous names in England. Thirty-three years ago in 1917, when my friendship with him just began, it was

already famous; already sprinkled with star dust, although at that time he had never set foot upon the professional stage apart from very occasionally, when he would appear at a charity performance looking extremely handsome and a little self-conscious to accompany some piercing soprano in one of her own compositions.

To sustain celebrity value for thirty-three years is a considerable feat. To sustain personal friendships for the same length of time through all the treacherous circumstances of continual success is even more remarkable. The answer, of course, lies in character. Ivor has a strong character; over and above the richness of his talent and the unquestionable force of his personality, he is determined, stubborn and industrious. He is also generous, kind and disarming; beneath several layers of superficial sentimentality, quite ruthless. Added to these paradoxical attributes he possesses what to my mind is the greatest gift of all, an indestructible sense of humour. This, generally directed against himself, is reserved for his personal life and is seldom apparent in public, for curiously enough, in spite of all his successful years, he is shy and self-conscious in front of strangers and, alas, in front of cameras. Apart from a few casual snapshots, I have never seen a photograph of him that gave the slightest indication of what he is really like. Before a camera his face takes on a set look, his eyes become soulful and frequently something quite dreadful happens to his mouth. He dons this lifeless *papier-maché* mask automatically on all public occasions. When perhaps in the cause of a charity he is brought forth or when he is face to face with a member of the Royal Family, his manner becomes strained and his fluid charm solidifies in an expression of miserable politeness. This startling transformation rarely takes place on the stage, although occasionally I have observed signs of it when for a few moments he has to remain static with nothing to do, I have observed it creeping up on him!

Another strange aspect of his character is his militant anti-snobbism. In his early years, several of his more blue-blooded admirers tore themselves to shreds in an effort to launch him socially. I believe that for a very brief period he partially succumbed and submitted himself to be taken to some of the more *recherché* non-theatrical parties of the period but it didn't last long. He was unimpressed and uncomfortable, the social jargon was alien to his ears and he was bored stiff and aching to get back to the warm, relaxed, theatrical cosiness of his own friends.

This undiminished, passionate love of his 'métier' is the most significant key to his character. Theatre, good, bad and indifferent, is the love of his life; to him other human endeavours are mere shadows.

Every now and then, spurred on by circumstances or doctor's orders, he journeys to some far off place, never alone, always surrounded by a group of his closest friends. Once there, he settles down to enjoy the climate and bask in the sun, always with the comforting thought at the back of his mind that he will soon be back in his dressing-room. Last year he spent a weekend in my home in Jamaica and we sat on the verandah in the lovely tropical evening light looking out over the mountainous coast, sodden with history and discussing with parochial intensity the return of Lily Elsie to the London stage in the nineteen-twenties.

For many years it has been fairly generally assumed that owing to the fact that both Ivor and I write plays and appear in them, we must inevitably be fierce rivals. Acquaintances who know neither of us well frequently attempt to curry favour by deprecating, usually very clumsily, either me to Ivor or Ivor to me. I warn these well wishers here and now in the coldest of cold print that they are wasting their time. Such a state of affairs never has existed and never will. To begin with, neither of us are temperamentally capable of professional jealousy and we are both far too occupied with doing what we want to do to worry about competition. We are both middle-aged, fortunate, talented and successful. We are both reviled by the Press and respected by the public. Above all, we like each other's company and have been close friends for over a quarter of a century. We have, of course, a lot in common. We were both boy sopranos and we both drink a lot of tea.

All this is a brief preface to the story of Ivor's life. I will add one more comment. The reward of his work lies in the fact that whenever and wherever he appears, the vast majority of the British public flocks to see him. He has provided romance, gaiety, nostalgia and pleasure for many millions of people for many years. He is also, among the few people who really know him, very much loved."

(1950)

*   *   *   *

CHAPTER FIVE

"DON'T YOU KNOW THERE'S A WAR ON?"*

1939·1945

London Pride has been handed down to us.
London Pride is a flower that's free.
London Pride means our own dear town to us,
And our pride it for ever will be.

("London Pride")

WHEN IT WAS SAFELY OVER, THERE WERE THOSE WHO SPOKE OF HAVING had 'a good war'. On the surface—and from his own published account—Noël had a frustrating one but previously classified papers are now coming to light that suggest there was rather more to it than he was allowed to say during his lifetime.

As soon as hostilities were declared, he took up a position in Paris as what was effectively head of propaganda. It was not a job that suited his particular talents, particularly when those first few months were so anti-climactic . . . "although there was a tremulousness in the air, a sense of unease, it was too vague to weigh heavily on people's spirits; in fact, it is questionable whether or not the large majority was even conscious of it. I was, or rather I like to believe that I was, but I am not sure . . . Looking back now on those strange, frustrating months, I find it difficult to believe that I ever lived them at all."

At Christmas 1939 he would express his feelings about the haphazard way we seemed to have drifted into disaster for the second time in his lifetime.

---

*Wartime catchphrase of British variety act, Hatton & Manners.

BACK TO THE NURSERY

Back to the Nursery,
Back to the Nursery,
Let us enjoy this sublime anniversary.
Full nineteen hundred and thirty-nine years
Let us forget the despair and the tears
Let us ignore all the slaughter and danger
(Think of the Manger! Remember the Manger!)
Let us envisage the Star in the East
(Man is a murderer. Man is a beast.)

Let us forget that the moment is sinister,
Let us uphold our devout Foreign Minister.
Let us not prattle of Simon or Hoare
Or Mr. Chamberlain's diffident war.
Let us not speak of Belisha or Burgin
(Think of the Virgin! Remember the Virgin!)
Let us from ridicule turn to Divinity
(Think of the Trinity! Think of the Trinity!)
Now as our day of rejoicing begins
(Never mind Poland. Abandon the Finns.)
Lift up your voices! "Long live Christianity!"
(Cruelty, Sadism, Blood and Insanity.)
So that the world across carnage is hurled,
God's in his Heaven—all's right with the world!

*   *   *   *

His duties in Paris brought him home on a regular basis and he found himself able to see his beloved London, that "grey city, stubbornly implanted" with new, more objective eyes . . .

LONDON 1940

"England is a good place to be just now. This may sound affected, almost bragadoccio, but for me it is true. These are dark hours and days and weeks and months that we are living through but the very dangers that surround us, the very fears and apprehensions that lie just below the surface of our ordinary lives give a certain zest to small pleasures which, in happier times, would have passed unnoticed.

How odd to be sitting below the house just before dawn with an overcoat on over your pyjamas, drinking a cup of tea and waiting for the 'All Clear' to sound! How strange, the casual, friendly conversations in dark streets; the feeling of comradeship with everybody; the little jokes! How strange and how comforting. It seems that for the first time people of all shapes and sizes and classes and creeds are getting to know one another. Never before, driving home snugly from theatres, restaurants, night-clubs or private houses, was there such richness, such awareness of adventure. Here we are on our little island and the issues have become simple. We have a good deal to grumble about, which is warming to the cockles of the spirit, like stamping the feet to keep out the cold.

Thousands of stories are exchanged all over the country during the strained hours of waiting. Gay stories, sad stories, personal experiences, criticisms of the Government, the Press, the A.R.P., the L.D.Vs, even the B.B.C. 'Careless talk', we are informed on all sides, may cost lives and aeroplanes and ships, so we dutifully bite back what we know to be an absolute fact, that a friend of ours heard from a friend of his who lives just near Dover that a friend of his saw with his own eyes a German plane disgorge seventeen real nuns dressed as Storm Troopers! We sometimes, of course, break down and whisper this but we are learning wisdom and so we leave out the fatal word 'Dover' and say 'Somewhere on the South East Coast' instead, thereby salving our national conscience and enhancing the mystery of our information,

London is emptier than I have ever known it. So many people have been evacuated to the country, so many mothers have taken or sent their children to the generous hospitality of the United States and Canada. As comparatively few Governesses and Nannys can be sent, many society ladies are thus enabled to get to know their children for the first time. The old order is certainly changing. The streets in the daytime look more or less normal, except for the nobler public buildings, such as the Houses of Parliament, Westminster Abbey and Claridges which are heavily sandbagged. Whitehall, Downing Street and all Government offices have, in addition to sandbags, complicated barricades of barbed wire and are sharply guarded, sometimes by veterans with fixed bayonets and a glint of Crimean reminiscence in their eyes, sometimes by very young men indeed who wear an expression of frightening zeal. Woe betide the eminent minister who has left his pass at the club.

In this building from which I am speaking, Broadcasting House, they are on the alert every hour of the day and night. It is comparatively easy to get in by the simple process of filling in a form at the desk; this form is duly stamped and handed to you. But getting out is quite another matter for, if you happen to drop or mislay your pass, you are incarcerated here for life! I have mine, at this moment, clutched firmly in my hand.

The spirit of the people is extraordinary. I have always had a romantic admiration for the common sense and courage of my countrymen and women. This admiration has occasionally shown itself in my writing. Perhaps in my adolescence during the last war, certain impressions became embedded in my subconscious mind. I was young then and paid little heed to what was going on but I suppose I knew, as we all knew, that we were in a tight corner. Now that I am older and have watched this danger growing year by year, until we find ourselves in the tightest corner we have been in for centuries, there is nothing subconscious about the impressions I am receiving.

The facts are clear and, as I said before, the issues are simple. We all know what we are up against and we are all prepared, united and unafraid—which is odd, for there is much to fear. In this fortitude which is neither stolid nor unimaginative there is a strong exhilaration. I became aware of it the moment I stepped out of the plane on my return from America four weeks ago. In the early months of the war there was a certain amount of fretfulness and scare, now there is none. Then there was uncertainty—now there is conviction.

In the year nineteen thirty-one on the opening night of *Cavalcade* I was called upon to make a speech in which I said that 'It was a pretty exciting thing to be English'. Later I regretted this. It seemed to me to have been too glib and theatrically patriotic. I regret it no longer, although now, of course, it almost belongs to the Understatement Department. I maintain that it is not only a pretty exciting thing to be English but essential as well, because on this side of the world it is all that there is left."

(BBC Radio Broadcast— 1 9 4 0)

*　　　　　*　　　　　*　　　　　*

For the men and women who would once more get us out of the trouble our statesmen had got us into he had nothing but total admiration.

THESE ARE BRAVE MEN

These are brave men
Who sail the sea in war
But we civilians must never mention it.
There's an unwritten law
That rules one multitude of ordinary heroes
To be prepared
Each minute of each hour
To stay at action stations
Closed in—sweating in the heat
To face much time
Far too much time
To wonder and to contemplate
In that long waiting,
So many possibilities to fear
To have, in convoying a Merchant fleet,
To move so slowly and to regulate
The engines of the ship, the nerves.
Each man's aware
In each man's secret heart
There lurks, not fright
But some dark premonition of what might
At any second happen.
Suddenly the ship swerves
Sharply to starboard—then again to port.
Submarine alarm
Enemy aircraft—bearing red 3.0
This may be it,
This may be the swift prelude to the slow
And sodden processes of dying.

By way of contrast, there were those who invoked his anger. One of them was Unity Valkyrie Mitford—errant sister of Nancy, Diana and Jessica, the 'Mitford Girls'. Her dubious claim to fame was her well-publicised affection for and association with Hitler and the leading Nazis.

In 1940 family pressure brought her reluctantly home from Germany. Noël was not about to allow her arrival to go unheralded . . .

NOTE ON OUR NEW NATIONAL HEROINE

Unity, Unity—Daughter of sorrow,
Creature of tragedy, child of distress,
Read her sad tale in the *Mirror* tomorrow,
Learn of her life in the *Daily Express*,
Think how she publicly postured and pandered,
Screeching her views on the Nazi regime.
Weep with her now in the *News* and the *Standard*,
Everything's over, the end of the dream.
Sigh for this amateur social Egeria,
Think how she suffered and suffered in vain,
Caught in the toils of neurotic hysteria,
Ne'er to take tea with her Fuhrer again.
No more photography—no more publicity,
No more defiance and devil may care.
Back to old England and bleak domesticity,
Nothing but decency, truth and despair.
No concentration camps—nothing exciting here,
Nothing sadistic. No national slaves.
Only the freedom for which we are fighting here,
Only Britannia still ruling the waves.
Unity—Unity—Daughter of sorrow
Sad, disillusioned and pampered and rich
How can she hope for a happy tomorrow?
What is there left for this tiresome bitch?

*   *   *   *

In mid 1940 Noël was rescued from his abortive Paris mission and sent to New York to sound out feeling in the then neutral USA. ("I was sent over by the Ministry of Information to work at gauging various cross sections of American opinion and reporting on it." Hard to conceive of it now, but it was by no means sure at the time that America would throw in its lot with the Allies—and, indeed, it was not to do so for nearly another two years.

Piecing the new facts together with the old account, it becomes clear that Noël was recruited on that first visit to be an unofficial 'agent' by the then head of combined Intelligence, Canadian William "Little Bill" Stephenson with the collusion of Sir Robert Vansittart at the Foreign Office. Noël's correspondence with Vansittart reveals that he was working for him as early as 1938.

He was meant to travel anywhere and everywhere and pass the information back to his Controls in New York and London—until a large spoke was thrown in the wheel by no less a person than Winston Churchill. "A power greater than we could contradict has thwarted our intents," Stephenson cabled. The assignment was peremptorily cancelled

One explanation is that the old man failed to see that visibility is its own best disguise. An emerging alternative is that he took a personal stand to distract enemy attention from Noël's activities, while tacitly allowing them to continue during the endless but less publicised troop tours that followed. Certainly, at the end of the war the Nazi "hit list" had Noël's name near the top of it. When it was published, his friend and fellow writer Rebecca West wrote to him—"My dear, the people we should have been seen dead with!"

Even when the war was long over, the Official Secrets Act prevented Noël from revealing his part in the war effort. In fact, it was not until the last year of his life—when he was being interviewed for a Canadian Broadcasting Company TV documentary on Stephenson—that he felt able to speak freely.

He recalled the 1940 New York meeting when he was first officially recruited.

"I was awfully bewildered. I thought it would be more Mata Hari—and then I told myself, 'Well, hardly that. I couldn't wear a jewel in my navel, which I believe she was given to doing . . .

"My celebrity was wonderful cover. So many career intelligence officers went around looking terribly mysterious—long black boots and sinister smiles. Nobody ever issued me with a false beard. And invisible ink ? I can't read my own writing when it's supposed to be visible. My disguise was my own reputation as a bit of an idiot.

"In the United States I just talked about Britain under bombing. Some of those senators—one or two who thought we were finished—did accuse me of being a spy. I said I would hardly be spying on my own people. But then in Latin America, I reported directly to Bill Stephenson while I sang my songs and spoke nicely to my hosts. A whole lot of tiny things are the stuff of intelligence. Smallest details fit into a big picture, and sometimes you repeat things and wonder if it's worth it. I travelled wherever I could go—Asia and what was left of Europe. And I ridiculed the whole business of intelligence, because that's the best way to get on with it—ridicule and belittle ourselves, and say what an awful lot of duffers we are, can't get the facts straight, all that sort of thing . . .

"I learned a lot from their technical people, became expert, could have made a career in espionage, except my life's been full of enough intrigue as it is."

*   *   *   *

Before he left his duties in the US at Churchill's behest, Noël prepared a broadcast to the American audience it was vital to persuade. The heading suggests it may never have been actually delivered . . .

INTENDED AMERICAN BROADCAST

"I would like to preface this talk with a personal note, a brief explanation of my attitude of mind in the face of the disaster which has come, not only upon my own country, but upon the entire civilised world.

A writer's first duty is to learn as much as he can about all aspects of human life and a few years ago I decided that, although I had acquired a pretty expert knowledge of my own profession, the Theatre, had travelled a good deal and mixed with many different sorts of people, that this wasn't enough. The game of politics was being played all round me, my own future and the future of everything I knew and believed in was being shaped and decided by groups of men in my own and other countries about whom I knew nothing.

A short man with a large head called Mussolini had made travel to Italy a great deal more comfortable, except that you were forbidden to put your feet up on the seats of railway carriages: in Germany there had been some sort of a fire in a Government building and another short man with an obvious strain of pathological fanaticism had been made Chancellor. At home in England a much larger man, Mr. Baldwin, smoked a pipe and was Prime Minister. Beyond these superficial facts I knew little of the forces at work, the preliminary rehearsals for the greatest tragedy the world had ever known. Since then I have made it my business to learn much and the more I have learned with my mind the heavier my heart has become.

I have watched, year by year, Democratic Governments ignoring the obvious signs and portents and ignoring not only signs and portents but actual, accurate information. I have listened to speeches and read of the signing and breaking of treaties. I have heard and read the warnings of Mr. Winston Churchill and discovered to my horror that many of those in high places who were in the position to take immediate action merely dismissed his eloquent prophetic words as alarmist warmongering. The culmination of this blindness and foolish apathy is now upon us and, as is usual with the strange race to which I belong, the ordinary peace-loving people are the ones who, with their backs to the wall, are valiantly fighting to the Death.

Of the ultimate outcome of this war I have not the slightest doubt. I know English people, I know what they believe in and why they are fighting. In the last War when bands played and flags blew in the wind the issues were less clearly defined. Their heroism then was for King and Country. An Ideal as limited as this sounds almost paltry with the weight of years upon it, but it was far from paltry: with the help of our allies in Europe and here we were fighting, under that particular guise, for the same thing for which we are fighting now, but then, as I said before, the issues were less clearly defined. Now we know.

This is no longer England's war, it is not even a new war, it is a continuation of the struggle between two cultures. Some wars have had no result beyond the destruction of life and wealth and happiness: others have diverted the course of history a trifle but have been soon forgotten, but a few have been determining factors in the history of civilisation. These latter are the wars in which two utterly opposed views of life have met and clashed. Such was the war between Persia and Greece in the fifth century B.C., and the war between Rome and Carthage two hundred and fifty years later. If Xerxes or Hannibal had been successful, the course of civilisation would have been changed. It is not two people or two Empires who now face each other, it is two views of life struggling for the control of the future.

This is one of the rare wars in history when the stake is not merely national or Imperial power, but the future development of mankind. If England loses this war she will cease to be a Great Power. Our links with the overseas world will be cut and we shall be obliged for the future to do what Germany tells us. Our position and dependence on food from abroad puts us utterly at the mercy of any power that rules the seas. But our own downfall will only be part of the downfall of the civilised world. A new ideal will determine not only the destiny of Europe but the destiny of the Americas as well and that ideal will be based on Force, Domination and ruthless brutality to all those of alien blood or different creeds: in fact, Nazism.

Nazism rejects all belief in the brotherhood of man; its idea of humanity consists of one ruling race and a number of other races naturally and eternally inferior.

It is still, in certain sections of the United States, considered farfetched even to visualise the possibility of Nazi domination here. I have heard many intelligent Americans argue clearly and concisely that such a situation could never possibly exist. I have also heard, before and during the war, Scandinavians, Dutch, Belgians, French and Englishmen use relatively the same arguments. Europe, of course, is far away, the wide ocean separates it from you. Japan is far away too, a wide ocean separates you from that, but there is no ocean wide enough to separate you from an epidemic and Nazism and Fascism combined contributes the most formidable infection that has ever threatened mankind.

An important issue in this country seems to be whether you declare war or not—surely this particular phrase has, during the last few years, become merely academic. Japan certainly never declared war on China and, as we all know, Germany has monotonously been declaring peace on everybody since nineteen thirty-six. As far as I can see, the United States is at war now and has been for several months. The fact that American men are not actually fighting with their bodies and muscles and blood doesn't signify nearly as much as the fact that millions of American men and women, writers, actors, radio announcers, journalists, even politicians are fighting now with their minds, voices and brains and have been doing so for a considerable while.

This War, contrary to much pessimistic belief, is not going to be won by force alone. It is going to be won by conviction, belief in the

Democratic way of life, and courage, not merely physical courage but moral courage and the personal incentive to utilise it, which incentive is still, thank God, a live and vital part of our heritage.

In my travels about this country lately I have never heard one American man, woman or child, however opposed to war they were, profess anything but loathing for the Nazi regime. I know, of course, that there are many thousands of German descent and sympathies that must feel it is a fine thing but it is odd that one never hears them say so openly. If they or those they have converted admire the ideals and methods of Hitler and his henchmen, their admiration is carefully obscured under protests against war—isolationism—parlour communism and countless other disguises. Who, in this great free territory, would dare to come out in a leading article or broadcast and claim that Adolph Hitler was the saviour of mankind and that they were prepared to support him in every way in their power? Who, in Pittsburgh—San Francisco—Des Moines—Chicago or New York would have the courage to organise a vast charity benefit for the war sufferers in Germany? Who indeed? Obviously no one, because they know perfectly well that they would probably be lynched if they did. In strict neutrality charitable assistance to the sufferers in belligerent nations should be impartial. Which, among all the humane charitable war organisations in this country, is publicly sending aid to Germany, Italy, Russia or Japan? The answer is not one, for the simple reason that the spirit and temper of these United States is as definitely opposed to Nazi domination as we are in England, and the small percentage who are not forced by the weight of public opinion to use the underhand insidious methods of pacifism and subversive political propaganda in order that their voices may be heard at all.

Taking all this into consideration—and I honestly and sincerely believe it to be true—where is the sense of all these shrill rhetorical questions as to whether America is coming into the War or not? The ardent and, I fear, slightly confused pacifists, can be silenced or not, as the case may be, by the single statement that of course America is not coming into the War for the sound reason that she is in it already in spirit, heart and mind and has been since the invasion of Finland.

We in England are at this moment fighting with all the force of arms that we have, which is not as much as we would like it to be, but the other force with which we are fighting and which will ultimately win, is indestructible. We are fighting not only physically to defend our country from the concrete horrors which are all too clearly dominating on the Continent, we are also defending the decency, justice, morality and freedom of the English speaking world without which life would be for me, and for you, unendurable."

(1940)

There was one other aspect of Noël's American tour of duty that went unnoticed. While being 'Noël Coward' was a perfect cover for a spy—an impersonation he was to use with brilliant effect when he played Hawthorne, the man from M.I.5, in the film of Our Man In Havana *(1959)—he felt that he had one more potent weapon in his professional armoury that could be deployed in the war effort. Or rather, in the effort to engage America in the war.*

He would write a play as propaganda.

Time Remembered *was written in early 1941. Set in Norma Ryerson's luxury home somewhere in Connecticut, it assembles a diverse group of people who represent different points of current opinion about the conflict in Europe. Most of them—including some longterm British expatriates like Maxwell (Maxie) Drage—are trying their best to ignore it and carry on with their sybaritic lifestyles.*

Into their midst arrives an old friend, Lelia Heseldyne, an English woman who, for the safety of her two sons, has brought them away from the bombing. At the time she and her husband had thought it the sane and safe thing to do but, as soon as she arrives and senses the attitudes of people she thought she knew, she begins to doubt it.

Noël describes her as . . .

". . . a woman of great personal charm; attractive, chic and typical of what is known as 'The International Set'. She is witty and articulate and has more intelligence than most of her kind. Her age is about forty. For the last so many years she has accepted the values of those with whom she has mixed but not quite unquestioningly, because her own innate personal honesty with herself, at moments, causes her, most uncomfortably, to see through the whole business. Instead of utilising this intuition and really getting down to brass tacks, she has allowed herself to drift with the tide—with the result that she is a good deal more unhappy than she allows anyone to suspect."

Maxie asks her about the crossing . . .

LELIA: We had a ship's concert too, highly patriotic, the Chief

Steward sang 'There'll Always Be An England' and we all joined in the chorus. I let the boys stay up and they adored it.

MAXIE: I suppose there will, won't there?

LELIA: Will what?

MAXIE: Always be an England?

LELIA: Really, Maxie, I'm ashamed of you—you must be out of your mind.

MAXIE: Lots of people over here doubt it very strongly, you know.

LELIA: They probably do, but they're quite, quite wrong. As a matter of fact, I don't see how they could be expected to know, really. They're a long way off and those sort of things can't be explained by the Press and the Radio—a few hours in a London air raid would convince them all right.

MAXIE: I didn't mean that *I* had any doubts, really—but it does get you down a bit, listening to people talk.

LELIA: Well, don't let it.

The rest prattle on in their usual inconsequential way, as if nothing had changed. For them it is inconceivable that America could enter the war . . .

NORMA: Isn't Andy and Marion's house enchanting? I think being right on the edge of the water like that is such an advantage, because even in the most sweltering weather you can always get a breeze—and that lovely view across to Long Island . . .

MARION: We're going to build on a big sort of playroom next spring—right at the end where the loggia is now—Bunny, you must come and help me with it . . .

BUNNY: I should adore to.

ANDY: If we're not in the war by next spring.

NORMA: Oh, Andy, I'm sure we shan't be—even if Roosevelt got in again and tried with all his might and main—the country would never stand for it. Of course, if he *does* get in, we shan't any of us have any money left, so nothing will matter anyway—Edward said to me just before he left for Florida— 'A Third Term and I go out of business automatically!' You

see, we obviously shouldn't be able to keep up this house, or
Sutton Place—we should just have to stay at the Waldorf for
a few months every year and travel for the rest of the time.

MELODY: But my dear, *where* could you go? There isn't anywhere left
to travel to.

LINDSAY: See America and die!

NORMA: (*Irritably*) Really, Lindsay, you know perfectly well that's not
the point at all. After all, we all love our country and are
proud of it—it is the last refuge of peace and freedom in the
world today—but you must admit that, once you've
exhausted Palm Beach and California, there aren't many
places to go!

LINDSAY: It would be a big pioneer step to start exhausting Arizona.

CHUCK: You've got something there, Lindsay—let's start now.

BUNNY: Alaine van Holt spent all last winter in Texas and said it was
heaven, but then she likes horses.

*Two of the other guests symbolise opposing points of view about the war and
the combatants. Rory Macullum, a failed novelist and successful drunk, is
critical of the Allies and of the 'beaten' French in particular. One evening
he and Marcel Thevelin, a supporter of the Free French cause, come to
blows. Norma is less concerned about the issues than about the lack—as she
sees it—of social manners. But the incident brings a lot of other things to
a head . . .*

MAXIE: Now then, Norma—don't get worked up again.

NORMA: I'm not in the least worked up. I'm merely utterly
disgusted. When people are under my roof I expect them
to behave in a civilised manner, not like hooligans. I can't
bear violence and vulgarity, it makes me physically ill—it
always has.

LELIA: Marcel Thevelin is neither vulgar nor uncivilised, Norma;
on the contrary he is an extremely intelligent and distin-
guished man and he came to dine with you tonight naturally expecting to be treated as such, instead of which he was
consistently insulted by one of your guests from the
moment he set foot in the house.

NORMA: My dear Lelia, I really don't see . . .

LELIA: (*Quietly*) I know the whole business has been very upsetting for you and I agree that it was most unpleasant but I would like you to see that in taking up the attitude you have over it, you really have got hold of the wrong end of the stick.

NORMA: I merely maintain that if you can't have a friendly discussion without coming to blows . . .

LELIA: It was *not* a friendly discussion.

NORMA: The fact remains he is staying in my house and he has a perfect right to say what he pleases.

LELIA: Does that apply to all of us?

NORMA: (*Horrified at LELIA's tone*) Why, Lelia?

LELIA: Because if it does, I have a few things I should like to say.

NORMA: Darling, you're over-tired—for heaven's sake let's not argue any more—let's play a nice word game or something . . .

LELIA: I'm not in the least over-tired.

NORMA: You've been in a very strange mood ever since you arrived, darling, we've all noticed it.

LELIA: You were quite right—it was because I was trying to make adjustments that weren't worth making.

NORMA: (*With a false laugh*) I wish I knew what you were talking about, Lelia, dear.

LELIA: I don't suppose you ever will really, but my conscience wouldn't allow me to leave your house without explaining—

NORMA: Leave my house! What on earth do you mean?

LELIA: I'm leaving your house tomorrow morning for the excellent reason that I couldn't bear to stay in it a moment longer.

NORMA: (*Furiously*) Well, really . . . I'm sure I don't know what *I've* done that you should turn on me like this.

LELIA: You haven't done anything, Norma. You never have done anything of the least significance or importance in your whole life. Neither have I, neither have most of the people we know. And now something is being done for us—something tremendous and violent and quite inexpressibly vulgar. There's a war on, Norma! I grant you it's inconvenient and a grave bore, because already it's interfering with our pleasures. But it's going to do worse than that before it's over, much worse.

NORMA: I think you must have gone mad, Lelia—I really do. You must be going to have a nervous breakdown.

LELIA: There's no longer any time for nervous breakdowns—I find that strangely comforting.

NORMA: I still don't understand why you should attack *me*. I mind about the war just as much as you do—and I've worked like a slave from morning till night ever since it started. Bunny will bear me out—I've done nothing but organise things and serve on committees until I've worn myself out . . .

LELIA: You don't even know what the war's about, Norma. You haven't the faintest conception of the issues at stake. If you had any real understanding of what is going on in these dangerous, tragic years, what took place tonight could never possibly have happened.

NORMA: So it was all my fault, was it? Well, I must say—

LELIA: It was *entirely* your fault—and if there's a rousing scandal about it—which I should think is highly probable—it will serve you right.

NORMA: How dare you speak to me like that, Lelia?

LELIA: I am speaking like this because I want there to be no confusion in your mind, no misunderstanding at all as to why I am going away. I am going because I find that we no longer have anything in common and because the atmosphere in this house of muddled thinking and false values is intolerable to me.

Lelia leaves her boys with another friend and sets off back to England to see the war through at her husband's side.

    Time Remembered *was never performed—for the simple reason that time overtook it. On December 7th, 1941 the Japanese attacked Pearl Harbor, Hawaii and all the arguments were over. America entered the war.*

*   *   *   *

For the rest of the war Noël travelled to wherever the armed forces were—along with almost every able-bodied entertainer, as well as many rather less well qualified.

Although he insisted on arranging his own tours, most of the rest fell under the auspices of ENSA (the Entertainment National Service Association), popularly referred to as "Every Night Something Awful". Ironically, the man in charge was Basil Dean, who had directed several of Noël's pre-war plays, including Easy Virtue *and* Home Chat.

Noël encapsulated his feelings about the organisation and the questionable nature of wartime entertainment in a sketch and accompanying song . . .

GOOD BYE, OLD FRIEND

The scene is a luxurious bedroom in the West End of London. MARION GAYE, *in an elaborate negligée is lying on a chaise-longue.* ELSIE SIMPSON, *wearing a tweed coat and skirt, is sitting on a chair beside her with a note book on her knee.*

MARION: It was a most wonderful, wonderful experience!

ELSIE: It must have been.

MARION: I shall never never forget it until the end of my days—those eager, loving faces—that pathetic gratitude—some of the boys, in the forward areas you know, actually broke down and cried.

ELSIE: *(Scribbling in shorthand)* "Broke down and cried."

MARION: They said that I reminded them of home *(She adjusts one of her diamond bracelets)*

ELSIE: *(Scribbling)* "Reminded them of *home*."

MARION: The conditions, of course, were unbelievable—fortunately, I don't mind roughing it—but still—*(She gives a gay little laugh)*

ELSIE: What sort of conditions?

MARION: (*Sweetly but sadly*) My dear—War is a grim business, you know.

ELSIE: Yes, I know—I was a Wren for three years—quite a lot of that time was spent at sea. I was torpedoed twice—

MARION: How *tremendously* interesting!—Where were we?

ELSIE: You were saying about the conditions being unbelievable.

MARION: I remember once giving a show in a rest camp—somewhere in Italy—and it started to rain in torrents—I assure you the skies literally opened.

ELSIE: Was the stage under cover?

MARION: (*Gently*) It had to be because of the piano and the microphones.

ELSIE: I see. Which did you find the best audiences, the Navy, the R.A.F or the Army?

MARION: Honestly, I couldn't say—they were all equally absolutely wonderful. Believe me, it was the most supreme experience of my whole life—and so deeply moving. Do you know that sometimes, when the show was over, some of them used actually to try and touch me.

ELSIE: How much did you give them?

MARION: You don't understand, my dear. They just wanted to touch my sleeve or my hand—they felt that overwhelming urge for a personal contact with someone from that England they loved so well.

ELSIE: (*Scribbling*) "England they loved so well"—My Editor wanted to know if you had any intimate, human experiences—

MARION: The whole tour was the most moving, intimate, human experience of my whole career. It was quite quite wonderful.

ELSIE: Yes, but did you meet anyone suddenly that you hadn't seen for years—did any faces from the past suddenly clutch at your heartstrings?

MARION: Well, there was General Hoskins—he was an angel—and darling Air Marshall Rogers—Sir Philip Rogers you know—I knew him before the war at Frinton.

ELSIE: (*Persistently*) But among the other ranks—did you find anyone you knew among the ordinary soldiers or sailors or airmen?

MARION: *(Beautifully)* I knew them all, my dear—I know that sounds a little foolish but I am sure you know what I mean—they were all near to me and so very, very dear to me—sometimes while I was singing I would suddenly see a face, just one face among all those thousands, staring at me with such a curious expression.

ELSIE: What sort of expression?

MARION: I don't know—those things are impossible to explain—sort of wistful I suppose—

ELSIE: Were you in danger at any time?

MARION: *(With a silvery laugh)* My dear—what a silly question—of course I was—incessantly.

ELSIE: I mean from enemy action?

MARION: *(Quietly)* I was nearly shot down in the desert.

ELSIE: During a performance?

MARION: *(With an acid little laugh)* My dear Miss Simpson, I think this little talk has really lasted long enough now, don't you? I'm dreadfully tired and I have an early rehearsal in the morning—I know you will understand.

ELSIE: *(Rising)* Of course. Thank you for giving me so much time.

MARION: *(Calling)* Eloise! *(To Elsie)* You must come and see me again when the play has opened—we'll have a little lunch together or something.

(ELOISE, *Marion's maid comes in*)

Eloise—Miss Simpson is leaving now.

ELSIE: I had a splendid interview with Dora Carstairs on Tuesday—she's been doing all the hospitals you know.

MARION: Poor sweet old Dora—such a tiny voice.

ELSIE: She's been doing it steadily for two and a half years.

MARION: Lucky creature to be able to get away.

ELSIE: Well, goodbye—and thank you again.

MARION: *(As they shake hands)* Goodbye. Remember me to your Editor, won't you?

ELSIE: *(Smiling)* I most certainly will.

(She goes, followed by Eloise. Marion strides irritably about the room. In a moment Eloise comes back)

MARION: If that bitch comes near me again, throw her out on her ear.

ELOISE: Yes, Miss Gaye.

MARION: *(Passing her hand wearily across her forehead)* Leave me now for a little, Eloise—I want to be alone

ELOISE: Yes, Miss Gaye.

(She goes out. Marion goes slowly over to a small trunk down Right. She opens it and takes out, very tenderly, her E.N.S.A. uniform. Kneeling there wistfully, with the uniform lying across her hands, she begins, brokenly, to sing.)

GOODBYE, OLD FRIEND

We've had good times,
You and I, you and I.
Now comes the moment
When we must say "Goodbye".
The hour chimes
From the East and from the West
And so I know,
And so I know
That I must sadly lay you down to rest.

Goodbye, old friend.
We've had our fill of it
We've known the thrill of it
Undismayed
For when the bugle called us, we obeyed.
Upheld by Rudyard Kipling, the *Express* and
Cavalcade.
To do or die, old friend.
That was the best of it,
We stood the test of it
To the end,
All set to play the final scene, no matter what befell

With Aspirin and Benzedrine and Mothersill as well.
We pledged ourselves to Basil Dean and followed him
        through hell!
Goodbye, old friend.

We've played our part
You and I—You and I
Adventure beckoned
Beneath the open sky
With heavy heart
I can tell—I can tell
The hour has struck
When I must whisper low 'Old Pal—Farewell'

Goodbye, old friend.
Though stormy weather blew,
We've been together through
Hail and snow.
When sometimes men stampeded from the show,
We didn't want to lose them but we knew they had
        to go.
Morale was high, old friend—
We sort of heightened it
Though we were frightened it
Might descend.
While driving through a coastal town in Southern
        Italy
Three stalwart groups of German troops emerged from the
        debris,
They saw the E.N.S.A. uniform and plunged into the
        sea!
Goodbye, old friend

(While she is singing this refrain the lights dim. From far away comes the sound of marching feet and also the sound of voices singing. They grow louder and louder and then, at the back, as though in a dream, she sees a vision of the E.N.S.A. boys and girls marching to victory.)

March—March—March
Fighting for E.N.S.A.
March—March—March
Fighting for Dean.
Though our jokes worry the censor
We try to keep the party clean.
We firmly shall
Uphold morale,
No matter if we flop
We'll never, never stop
Amusing the troops until they drop.
With might and main
Singing a glad refrain—
Fighting for E.N.S.A., Dean and Drury Lane.

March—March—March
Fighting for E.N.S.A.
March—March—March
Follow the drum.
Though the crowds might have been denser
Not all the troops are all that dumb,
When all this ends
And bitter friends
Say "Tell us furthermore,
Apart from one encore,
Just what did you do to win the war?"
With pride serene
We shall reply "We've been
Fighting for E.N.S.A., Drury Lane and Dean.

(The vision fades and once more she is alone with her memories)

Goodbye, old friend.
We learned the trick of it,
Right in the thick of it ,
Wet or fine.
From Burma to the forests of the Rhine
The men who heard us couldn't wait to get back to
         the line.
We'd bravely try, old friend,

Ways of controlling them,
Means of cajoling them
To attend.
When during one performance someone hissed and
    threw a stone,
I flung my N.A.A.F.I. sandwich down and seized the
    microphone
And shouted "God for Harry Roy—Geraldo—and
    St.Joan!"
Goodbye, old friend.

      *   *   *   *

In 1945 it was all over and he could reflect on what the war had achieved. His feelings about the future that faced England were not nearly as optimistic as they had been in 1940 . . .

VICTORY?

"During the years of peace, in that other life that we have almost forgotten; luxurious British commercial liners—without fear of night attack, U-boats, bombs or torpedoes—used to ply to and fro across the seven seas. It was a convention in these ships, an unwritten law, that on the last evening before the end of the voyage there should be a disciplined celebration, ' The Captain's Dinner'. On these occasions the stewards solemnly placed balloons, rattles, squeakers, crackers and little net bags of coloured paper balls on every table; the ship's' orchestra played gay tunes with verve and a certain valedictory abandon, and the passengers, many of whom had not spoken to one another throughout the trip, surrendered obediently to the 'gala' atmosphere, ordered more wine than usual, pulled the crackers, donned the paper caps, exploded the balloons with cigarette-ends, whirled the rattles, blew the squeakers and vivaciously hurled handfuls of the coloured paper balls into the faces of complete strangers.

We are a law-abiding, docile people; orders are orders, and it was 'The Captain's Dinner'. We are still, in spite of the ordeals we have endured, a law-abiding , docile people; orders are still orders, and it is 'Victory Day'. A day which, after years of tragedy, defeat, suffering, humiliation, fortitude and imperishable courage, has at last dawned for us. Having agreed to write an article commemorating this tremendous occasion I find myself faced with an insuperable obstacle and that obstacle is that I don't believe it.

'Victory Day!' The slogan seems too facile, its implications too final and too absolute. One day set apart in time, presumably to be revived year after year *ad infinitum*: one day bracketed annually for legitimate exultation: out with the flags, rattles, squeakers and paper caps—here we are again—let's have a party and remember and get drunk and try to forget. The voyage is over, or rather the first part of the voyage is over: perhaps we can afford to be noisy and a little silly: surely we have reason enough for celebration? Perhaps we may be forgiven if we cheer and shout and throw our paper caps in the air. The relief is immense. We can go to sleep in peace. There will be no more ear-splitting sirens to drag us awake: no more impersonal violence and sudden fear: no more urgent demands made upon our courage and endurance and will to survival. We can, as Fred Astaire once sang, 'Pick ourselves up, dust ourselves down and start all over again!'

At least it looks as if we can. The skies are clear: all our elderly gentlemen are full of promises and our soldiers, sailors and airmen, some of them, will be coming home again. Certainly on the face of it we have enough reason for celebration, or at any rate for tentative celebration but somehow the word Victory seems too overwhelming, too complete and surely a great deal too premature. We have conquered the Nazis in war; defeated their armies on land, their ships on the sea and their Luftwaffe in the air. Their ambition to dominate the world, to impose their 'new order' of tyranny and subjugation upon free peoples has been shattered. The might and determination of the united Nations has forced them back into their battered and devastated Fatherland, where presumably, all they have left to do is to lick their wounds and howl for mercy. It is certainly victory over the Nazis and deserving of a few flags and bugles, but the triumph is not final. We have not yet conquered the Japanese, and it remains to be seen whether or not we have really conquered the Germans!

Above all, and before our victory can be set in history whole and complete, we shall have to do a little conquering of *ourselves*. This is indeed a great opportunity, probably the greatest our country has ever had. For five dreadful years the people of Britain have endured intense personal suffering and loss, and the violence of air bombardment on their undefended cities. They have also, and this has perhaps been more difficult, put up cheerfully with the countless minor discomforts of war: food, fuel and clothes rationing; fewer and fewer transport facilities; the soul-destroying, endless dreariness of the black-out; the months of anti-climax when apparently nothing was happening at all and the end of the war seemed so far away as to be almost inconceivable.

All this has been endured with stoicism and our deep-rooted, indestructible humour, and it has, of course, done us a power of good. Archaic class distinctions have been broken down; the poor are no longer the poor, the rich are no longer the rich and the middle classes (always the most rigid social autocrats) have sent their insular prejudices whistling down the wind and relaxed into an unselfconscious gregariousness from Cheltenham to Maida Vale and from Kensington to Peckham Rye: they have even, since the influx of American and Dominions troops, been known to speak to strangers in railway carriages. In addition to these marked improvements in our national character there appears to be on the part of most people a healthy desire to participate in the affairs of the country, a desire which was dismally lacking in the black years immediately preceding the war. We have assuredly learned a lot but our victory will not be proved and consolidated unless we have learned enough; and I hope, I so profoundly hope that we have.

Speaking personally, I know that during this war I have been more fortunate and privileged than most civilians. I have travelled many hundreds of thousands of miles and have had the opportunity of watching events from many different angles. I have returned to this country several times, stayed awhile and then gone away again and have therefore, I think, been able to see the various moral and psychological changes in clearer perspective than those who have remained at home all the time. Above all I have been lucky enough to have been in close contact over and over again with the men who are fighting for us. Being neither a statesman, a politician, a government official, a military strategist nor even a journalist my observation has been untrammelled by any particular urgency or prejudice. This perhaps is sufficient reason for me to tell you a little of what I have learned about ourselves as a nation and a Commonwealth of Nations in relation, not only to our enemies but to our allies as well.

It is time, I feel, for at least one Britisher to discard temporarily our age-old tradition of understating our achievements and I would like to warn any of my readers who still cherish intellectual illusions of world democracy and equality of nations and peace-in-our-time, that they are going to disapprove profoundly of what I am about to say.

First of all, I do not believe that genuine peace in our time is possible, probable, or in the long view, even desirable. If we grab too eagerly at peace in *our* time and compromise again with our ideals and betray again our warriors, there will be no hope of peace for our children or our children's children. The far future is more important than the immediate future; maybe not for us but certainly for those who follow after. The immediate future is more, much more important than the present and in this we can participate, for this we can work and try to see clearly and remain vigilant until the end of our days.

Let us, for God's sake, or rather for the future's sake, not be deceived by our Victory Day. The physical war is perhaps nearly over but the moral war is only just beginning. We as a race are capable, like all other races, of prevarication, muddled thinking, sentimentalism, untimely arrogance and most untimely self-deprecation but we are also capable, in adversity of greater qualities than any other race in the world. Must adversity always be our only spur? Can we not this time, with so many bitter lessons learned, be brave and strong and vigilant in comparative peace as well as in total war? Let us try with all our concentrated will to maintain the spirit that upheld us in 1940. Let us remember, disregarding political tact and commercial expedience, that it was our inherited, stubborn integrity that gave the future of the civilised world a chance and a glimmer of hope. It was our soldiers who fought on the land, our young airmen who cleared the skies and our sailors who kept the sea routes open. Then we had no allies. We had much sympathy from other parts of the globe and much sincere admiration but we had no allies and we stood alone in the path of the most powerful and menacing onslaught in the history of mankind. A menace not only to ourselves and our much decried British Empire, but a menace to all those who are now fighting side by side with us.

It may be considered by many 'bad taste' to emphasize so insistently this immeasurable achievement but we live in an age of advertisement, publicity and specialised propaganda and now, amidst the rather deafening cacophony of trumpets, one or two gentle fanfares on British bugles should not strike too sharp a discord. This is Victory Day but there were greater Victory Days in 1940 for us and for the world because then it was the beginning and now it is still a long way from the end."

*   *   *   *

This war's making most people feel bloody in one way or another—apart from the actual, immediate horror of it, it's planting a fine crop of neuroses in all of us. God knows what we shall be like when it's over.

— **Lelia** in *Time Remembered* (Unproduced play—1 9 4 1)

UNFINISHED BUSINESS

THE PLAYS

*   *   *   *

"Before the first word of the first act is written, the last act should be clearly in the author's mind, if not actually written out in the form of a synopsis. Dialogue, for those who have a talent for it, is easy; but construction, with or without talent, is difficult and is of paramount importance. I know this sounds like heresy in this era of highly-praised, half-formulated moods, but no mood, however exquisite, is likely to hold the attention of an audience for two hours and a half unless it is based on a solid structure."

(Future Indefinite)

IT'S HARD TO STATE CATEGORICALLY WHICH WAS THE FIRST NOËL COWARD play. While *The Rat Trap* was written in 1918, it was not produced until 1926—after the success of *The Vortex*—whereas *I'll Leave It To You*, though written a year later, was actually produced first in 1920.

And even that does not tell the whole story, for Noël's notebooks contain fragments of plays dating back to 1915, as well as lists of possible titles, notes on characters and snatches of dialogue. Whatever else was occupying him creatively, an idea for a play was never far away.

In the year of *The Rat Trap* he also wrote *The Last Trick* (which "wasn't particularly original but the dialogue was effective, and showed a marked improvement on my other work.") He also wrote "two bad plays"—

The Impossible Wife and *The Unattainable*, a play significant for the fact that it introduces us for the first time to a character called Elvira.

The tone in the handwritten manuscript (dated May 15th 1918) suggests *The Vortex* crossed with *Private Lives* . . .

THE UNATTAINABLE

MRS. HOUGHTON NAIGRILL: I rather agree with Elvira—it must be a wonderful sensation

MAJOR CARRINGTON: Damned unhealthy form of amusement, I call it.

MRS. HOUGHTON-NAIGRILL: One wouldn't expect a man like you to be in the least interested in drug taking, dear Major—It naturally appeals to the more degenerate natures.

NORMAN CRAST: I should love to try it.

LADY CARRINGTON: My dear boy, your panting efforts to be decadent are almost pathetic . . . you're foolish to endeavour to follow in the footsteps of your ancestors. In so many cases it's much more commendable to live down tradition than live up to it.

ALICE POTTINGE: Poor Norman, you're always snubbing him, Lady Carrington.

LADY CARRINGTON: I feel it my duty, being his only living Aunt.

IRENE COURTE: I should love to smoke just one little pipe of opium to see what happens.

KATT SAVILLE: You'd probably be able to obtain the same result by crossing the Channel on a rough day.

IRENE COURTE: Oh, how disgusting. But I'm really a splendid sailor.

MRS. HOUGHTON-NAIGRILL: I thought you said you'd never been further than Ryde?

(1918)

*   *   *   *

After the 1924 success of The Vortex, *Noël was inspired—during his US tour with the play—to attempt a successor, although it was in no way intended as a sequel. He wrote to his friend and fellow writer, Beverley Nichols . . .*

"The play I wrote was called *Semi-Monde* (originally *Ritz Bar*) and the whole action of it took place in the public rooms of the Ritz Hotel in Paris over a period of three years. It was well constructed and, on the whole, well written." . . . But he was in little doubt that "its production in London or New York seemed unlikely, as some of the characters, owing to some lightly suggested abnormalities, would certainly be deleted by the Censor."

There was serious talk of a Max Reinhardt production in Germany but the appearance of Vicki Baum's novel, Grand Hotel, *being—as Noël recognised—"too closely similar in theme" meant that* Semi-Monde *"faded gently into oblivion."*

(At least, it did for the next fifty years—at which point (1977) the Glasgow Citizens' Theatre produced it to a degree of critical acclaim and, in the afterglow of the Coward Centenary, there was a West End production in March 2001.)

Almost as soon as he had written the piece, Noël felt the need to write his apologia, *which incidentally expressed his views on the state of the post-World War I English theatre . . .*

PREFACE TO 'SEMI-MONDE'

I feel that a few words of explanation are necessary to exculpate *Semi- Monde* from the charges of 'licentiousness', 'decadence' and 'sensationalism'. Several times before with regard to my earlier plays these three qualities have been accredited to me in addition to several others equally vituperative. Therefore, in this case I wish to forestall the inevitable by laying at the disposal of whosoever cares to read it a brief outline of my real motives in writing of types and characters which, although constituting a comparatively small section of civilised society, are nevertheless just as valuable as factors in Human Drama as Gentlemen Burglars, Lancashire Homicides and Elizabethan Harlots.

At the time of writing this there is being waged in England a pas-

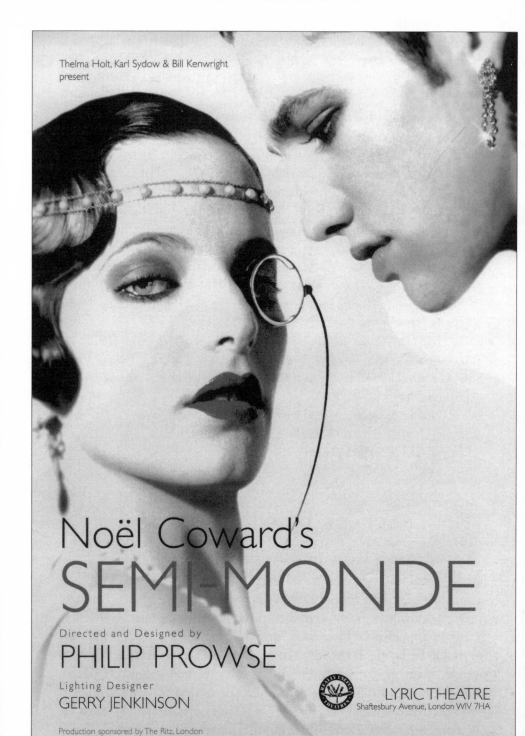

Thelma Holt, Karl Sydow & Bill Kenwright
present

Noël Coward's
SEMI-MONDE

Directed and Designed by
PHILIP PROWSE

Lighting Designer
GERRY JENKINSON

LYRIC THEATRE
Shaftesbury Avenue, London WIV 7HA

Production sponsored by The Ritz, London

sionate campaign against what are described as 'unpleasant' plays—that is plays which utilise (perhaps a little more frankly than usual)—conflicting sex relationships for the furtherance of their dramatic values. There have been several hysterical demands—generally, it must be admitted, from elderly clergymen in Norfolk—that sex be abolished from the stage altogether. This suggestion, though too fatuous to be considered seriously, serves to illustrate the distressing trend of public opinion at a moment when the British Drama is tottering so visibly that artificial restoration has to be resorted to in the shape of imported American farces and musical comedies in increasing numbers.

The British nation since its deliverance from the horrors of war in 1918 appears in its attitude towards art to have become more and more lethargic—a comatose smugness seems to have swept over the land. In other countries tremendous efforts are being made in the progress of literature and drama. And for each forward step registered in America, Germany, France or Italy, England falls back two, completely undismayed in its serene and idiotic complacency. The younger writers are forced to compromise, because in most cases they are not in a position to fight and have a living to make. The slightest break away from tradition is greeted with fear and suspicion by the Church and State. Sincerely written plays by unknown young authors are turned down in feverish haste by the Lord Chamberlain, thereby being denied the judgement of the public, which is after all their right, solely because—in many cases quite unwittingly—they present problems comic or tragic of the present day as contrasted with the standards of twenty-five years ago. These being unfortunately the only standard by which those in authority seem to be capable of judging.

During the years between 1914 and 1918 the general nerve tension was so great that with the sudden cessation of strain a complete psychological reaction was inevitable and it is in the midst of this reaction that we are living now. Moral values as they were have long since lost all significance. Ideals and ambitions as they were have changed likewise. This does not in any way mean abolishment, merely readjustment and it is this all important fact that the older generation seems incapable of grasping."

(1926)

*   *   *   *

In another letter to Nichols recalling the twenties Noël wrote:

> "Were we happy in the Twenties? On the whole I think most of
> us were but we tried to hide it by appearing to be as *blasé*, world-
> weary and 'jagged with sophistication' as we possibly could.
> Naturally we had a lot of fun in the process. I remember I had
> a lovely time writing a play called *Ritz Bar* which you, Beverley,
> most kindly tried to get the Norwegian Ambassador in Paris to
> back—why I can't think. Anyway, *Ritz Bar* was as jagged with
> sophistication as all get out; the characters were either demi-
> *mondaine* or just plain *mondaine*, shared their apartments and
> their lives with members of the opposite, or the same, sex and
> no wife dreamed for one instant of doing anything so banal as
> living with her husband. The play was typical of the phase we all
> went through and, taken by and large, quite harmless: to call it
> good clean fun would perhaps be going too far, but at least it
> wasn't about the Death Wish and compared with Existentialism
> it becomes *Rebecca of Sunnybrook Farm*."

*He didn't need to mention that in the character of Beverley Ford ("about
forty, extremely well dressed") he had even depicted his friend.*

*By that time he must have been aware of Nichols' description of him
in a 1927 feature article ("Celebrities in Undress") in* The Sketch
*as "clovenhoofed . . . a sentimentalist terrified of being found out—by
himself".*

*   *   *   *

*By the end of the war revue seemed to have played itself out—at least for
the time being. In a sense this was strange, since 'intimate revue'—
as opposed to the lavish girls-and-sets 'spectacular revue'—was comparatively economical to stage and would have seemed well-suited to the
austerity of the post-World War II West End.*

*There were, of course, isolated and honourable pockets of resistance
through the 1950s but then television took hold, learned that economic
lesson—and down came the final curtain.*

Noël's last revue was the 1945 Sigh No More, *which enjoyed a mod-
estly successful run. As was usual with the form, a great deal more material was written than was finally performed. One rather lavishly cast
sketch was "The Rest is Silence."*

THE REST IS SILENCE

The scene is the third floor landing of an English Nursing Home. There are three doors at the back numbered 13, 14 and 15. Off on the left is the patients' lavatory and bathroom and off on the right the nurses' pantry. The lift and staircase are off stage left.

On stage there is a small table with a few illustrated magazines on it. There are a few chairs. These are for the convenience of the visitors, but are used almost exclusively by the nurses.

When the curtain rises it is late afternoon.

> (SISTER FRISBY *is seated comfortably left reading a book. The red light above the door of Number 14 flicks on and off with a buzzer.* SISTER FRISBY *looks up at it disdainfully and continues to read.*)

> (SISTER HEWITT *comes in from the left with a large bunch of flowers and passes through to the pantry on the right.*)

SISTER H: *(As she goes)* More flowers for Number 12—you'd think she was the Queen of Sheba.

> (SISTER FRISBY *doesn't look up. The light above Number 14 goes on again. She pays no attention.* SISTER MUNRO *comes out of Number 15 carrying a utensil covered with a towel.* SISTER FRISBY *beckons to her and abstractedly, still reading, feels under the towel and produces a few grapes which she pops into her mouth. After this she dismisses* SISTER MUNRO *with a regal wave of the hand.*)

> (SISTER MUNRO *goes off*)

> (SISTER O'KEEFE *comes on and flings herself into a chair.* SISTER TRACY *enters*)

SISTER T: How's your patient, dear?

SISTER O'K: It's wailin' and roarin' like a banshee she is, I'd like to crack her one.

SISTER T: You look tired out, shall I get you a cup of tea?

SISTER O'K: It's something stronger than tea I'll be needin' after dealin' with that black-hearted old harridan.

> *(The light in Number 14 goes on again)*

SISTER T: *(To* SISTER FRISBY*)* That's yours, dear.

(SISTER FRISBY *gives her a withering look and goes on reading*)

(SISTER WEEVIL *comes out of Number 13 carrying a bow and arrow*)

SISTER T: Your tea's in the pantry, dear, I put a saucer on top to keep it nice and hot.

SISTER W: Thanks very much, I'm sure.

SISTER O'K: How is she?

SISTER W: Bright as a button. She's been Robin Hood all the afternoon, but she's tired of it now.

(*She goes off with the bow and arrow*)

(SISTER O'KEEFE *lights a cigarette. There is the sound of the lift door opening and* BERT, *the lift boy, enters carrying two dead pheasants*)

BERT: Couple of birds for Number 11—They stink 'orrible!

SISTER T: Oh, dear, whatever are we to do with them?

BERT: You could always wear them.

SISTER T: Hold your tongue, Mr. Sharp.

(BERT *goes off*)

(SISTER O'KEEFE *looks wistfully at the pheasants which he has placed on the table*)

SISTER O'K: Poor pretty creatures. To think that only a little while ago they were flyin' about free as the air, and look at the darlins' now.

(SISTER FRISBY *gives them a nasty look and ostentatiously moves to a chair on the other side of the stage.* SISTER RAWLINGS *comes in carrying a tea-tray*)

SISTER: What's that terrible smell?

SISTER T: Pheasants for Number 11

SISTER R: You'd better take them in and show them to him and then send them to the kitchen.

(*She goes off*)

SISTER O'K: (*Calling after her*) Is it His Holiness the Pope yer think y'are—giving everyone orders?

(SISTER WEEVIL *returns bearing a cup of tea.* SISTER HEWITT *follow her with the flowers in a vase*)

SISTER H: Same card, same handwriting, same message—'Bobsie Wobsie loves you'.

SISTER T: That ought to cheer her up and make her feel better.

SISTER H: (*Contemptuously*) Better! She's strong as a horse,lying there moaning on her lace pillows.

(*She goes off*)

(*The door of Number 13 opens gently and a little* OLD LADY *in a quilted dressing-gown comes out. She has a quill pen stuck in the back of her hair. She creeps up behind* SISTER WEEVIL *and, putting her finger in her mouth, gives an Indian call*)

SISTER W: (*Jumping*) My God!

OLD LADY: I'm Pocahontas—I'm Pocahontas!

SISTER W: (*Recovering herself*)   No you're not, dear, you're Mrs. Etheridge.

(*She leads her gently but firmly back into her room*)

(*The light on Number 14 goes on again.* SISTER FRISBY *gives it a baleful look, flings her book down and goes in. there is the sound of a slight scream. She comes out again, sits down, picks up her book and continues to read.* SISTER MUNRO *comes on and goes into Number 15.* SISTER WEEVIL *comes out of Number 13*)

SISTER W: It's all right—she's in bed again.

SISTER T: Funny the ideas she gets.

SISTER W. I don't know how she thinks of them, really I don't.

SISTER T: Well, I suppose it keeps her happy.

SISTER W: I don't mind when she's nice, quiet people like Voltaire or Emily Bronte, but I hope to God she's never Henry the Fifth again—it made such a racket!

(*There is the sound of loud laughter from Number 15.* SISTER FRISBY *looks up irritably from her book*)

SISTER T: Hark at Munro and Number 15—she'll get what for if Matron hears her.

SISTER O'K: She's light-minded that girl—it's sorrow in the future that she's layin' up for herself.

(SISTER MUNRO *emerges from Number 15 in fits of laughter. She is carrying some object under a towel*)

SISTER T: What on earth's the matter?

SISTER M: That man does the silliest things!

> (*She goes off still shaking with laughter*)

SISTER O'K: That girl ought only to be given stretcher cases, she's a walking peril to convalescents.

(SISTER RAWLINGS *returns*)

SISTER R: Why haven't those birds been taken away?

SISTER T: Leave them here a little longer and they'll go by themselves. (*She laughs delightedly at her own joke*)

(SISTER FRISBY *gives her a filthy look*)

(SISTER RAWLINGS *ignores the whole thing and goes out*)

(*The door of Number 13 opens again and the little* OLD LADY *comes out, this time she is precariously balancing a napkin ring on her head over a lace handkerchief. But she is also puffing out her cheeks*)

SISTER W: (*Seeing her*) Oh, you promised me you'd stay in bed—you are naughty!

OLD LADY: I'm Queen Victoria!

SISTER W: No, you're not, dear—you're Mrs. Etheridge.

> (*She wearily takes her back into her room*)

(*The buzzer and light over Number 14 goes on and off insistently.* SISTER FRISBY *disregards it for a little and then puts her book down with an expression of ill-concealed fury and goes off. In a moment she returns with a formidable-looking hypodermic syringe. She tests it with sinister thoroughness and vanishes into Number 14.*)

(SISTER MUNRO *comes gaily on with a bottle of champagne*)

SISTER M: (*Brandishing it*) Champagne wine—I'll thank you!

SISTER T: You know he oughtn't to have more than a sip once a day.

SISTER M: We're having a party—just a few friends and a Wurlitzer— pop in if you're passing.

SISTER O'K: You'll be havin' the sack, that's what you'll be havin'—

SISTER M: My dears, he's mad about me—it's *joie de vivre* that counts and don't you make any mistake about it. Madame Xenia said to me only last week—"You're naturally gay and spontaneous and you have nothing to fear—a dark stranger will cross your path and alter the whole course of your life!" This is him.

SISTER T: I suppose she didn't happen to mention that he had a glass eye?

SISTER M: (*Gaily*) Spoilsport!

(*She vanishes into Number 15*)

(SISTER WEEVIL *comes out of Number 12 and sits down wearily*)

SISTER W: Well, she's in bed again but there's no knowing how long she'll stay there. She's been more unsettled today than she has been for weeks. I had to pretend I was the Angel Gabriel before she'd let me out of the room.

SISTER T: How on earth did you do that?

SISTER W: (*Sipping her tea*) I just waved my arms, made believe they were wings—she loved it.

(*There is another cry from Number 14, then dead silence.* SISTER FRISBY *comes out, sits down and goes on with her book. Her expression is inscrutable. There's a burst of wild laughter from Number 15*)

SISTER T: One more glass of champagne and she'll be under the bed.

SISTER O'K: Or in it.

SISTER W: Sister O'Keefe, how *can* you!

SISTER O'K: It's getting us all into trouble she'll be after with her fast ways and her lipstick and her wicked sexy bedevilment.

SISTER T: (*In fits of laughter*) Oh, Sister O'Keefe, you kill me—honestly you do.

(*The* MATRON *enters. She is a woman of austere bearing and she wears pince-nez*)

MATRON: Sister Tracy, what are you laughing at?

SISTER T: Nothing, Matron—just a joke of Sister O'Keefe's.

MATRON: I'll trouble you, Sister O'Keefe, not to be amusing until you're off duty.

SISTER O'K: Mother of God, I never said a word.

MATRON: And don't blaspheme either. What's that horrible smell?

SISTER W: It's them pheasants.

MATRON: *Those* pheasants. Kindly have them sent to the kitchen at once—

(At this moment there is a louder burst of laughter from Number 15)

MATRON: Good Heavens!

SISTER M: *(She opens the door of Number 15. The noise continues at full pitch.* SISTER MUNRO's *voice is heard saying with shrill gaiety)*

Who do you think you are—Casanova?

SISTER: *(In thunderous tones)* Sister Munro!

(There is dead silence for a moment, then SISTER MUNRO *comes out. She is doing up the collar of her uniform and carrying her cap in her mouth)*

MATRON: What is the meaning of this?

SISTER M: I was just speaking to Mr. Meadows, he's very restless.

MATRON: You have been drinking!

SISTER M: He insisted on me having a drop—he did really.

MATRON: You are a disgrace to your profession—you are dismissed!

SISTER M: *(Truculently)* Oh, dismissed am I—we'll see about that.

MATRON: I have nothing further to say.

SISTER M: Who are you to talk, I'd like to know—you and Doctor Rogers!

MATRON: How dare you!

SISTER M: It's the scandal of the whole place—Doctor Rogers this and Doctor Rogers that and giving him sardines on toast at all hours of the night in your private sitting-room.

MATRON: Pack your things and leave.

SISTER M: I'll leave when I please—and don't you imagine that you can talk to me like that—

SISTER O'K: *(Simultaneously)* For the love of Heaven stop answering back, Munro—

SISTER T: *(Simultaneously)* I don't think she meant any harm, Matron, really I don't, it was Mr. Meadow's fault—you know what men are—

SISTER W: *(SImultaneously)* You haven't any right to talk to Matron in that tone and well you know it—

(*Pandemonium ensues and everyone talks at once.* SISTER FRISBY *takes no part in it, but continues to read her book*)

(*The door of Number 13 opens gently and the little* OLD LADY *comes out again. This time she is wearing a soft black hat and carrying a revolver. She takes careful aim and shoots, in turn,* MATRON, SISTER TRACY, SISTER OKEEFE, SISTER MUNRO *and* SISTER WEEVIL. *They all fall.*)

OLD LADY:(*Exultantly*) I'm Al Capone!—I'm Al Capone!

(SISTER FRISBY *rises with an expression of irritation and steps carefully over the recumbent bodies*)

SISTER F: (*As she goes*) No you're not, dear—you're Mrs. Etheridge!

*   *   *   *

*In the early 1960s—perhaps with a sense of time running out—Noël began to focus on the playwright in him. Of the material that was actually produced one show was a musical (*Sail Away—*1961) and another musical in which he was involved as director (*The Girl Who Came To Supper—*1963) also took up a disproportionate amount of his time and energy.*

The single straight play was the trilogy, Suite in Three Keys (1966) *in which Noël appeared himself and effectively said his goodbyes to the West End stage he loved so much.*

During these years, however, he started on many other projects. There was a full length adaptation of his own short story, Star Quality (1965)— *that dissection of the star actress as* monstre sacrée—*which is only now being produced thirty-five years later..*

There were, in addition, two other pieces of vintage—but sadly, unfinished—Coward.

A Diary *entry for February 19th, 1962 (Jamaica) outlines the first of them . . .*

"The principal event of the last week is that I have constructed a new comedy. The title for the moment, is *Three For The Money* and it is about a ramshackle Irish castle and a ramshackle Irish lord who has three beautiful but undisciplined daughters, upon whose charms he relies to save the family fortunes. An ex-mistress takes them off to France, educates them in the suitable graces and, in one way or another, they all manage to find rich gentlemen. At the end of the play they are all three, for various reasons, free of their encumbrances and ready to set forth on further adventures. Meanwhile, the house is restored and the family estate secured. This is a very bald outline but it offers opportunities, I think, for good comedy situations. I intend, if I can, to write it on a plane just above reality, as I did *Blithe Spirit*. If it comes down to solid ground for a moment it will disintegrate. I am looking forward to having a bash at it."

In the event all he wrote was the opening scene . . .

THREE FOR THE MONEY

ACT ONE, SCENE I

DAVINA: (*At the window*) The last time Father came home from prison it was raining. Isn't that a coincidence?

CANDY: It would be more of a coincidence if it wasn't at this time of year.

PENNY: (*At the mantlepiece*) Somebody's been at my Cadbury's nut-milk. There was more than half left when I hid it yesterday. Now there's only a tiny bit.

DAVINA: It serves you right for being furtive. Why didn't you stuff yourself openly! No one is deceived. Even the mice know.

PENNY: (*Looking ruefully at the remains of her chocolate bar*) This was no mouse. It's been cleanly broken and there are no tooth marks. (*She eats what is left.*)

CANDY: You'll grow as fat as a pig and have to wriggle yourself into tight girdles and nobody will desire you.

PENNY: Oriental gentlemen might. Oriental gentlemen are crazy for fatness and swelling voluptuous curves.

DAVINA: Oriental gentlemen are few and far between in Ireland, even during Horse Show week.

PENNY: In that case I shall make a bee line for Istanbul

(*Aunt Hattie comes in*)

HATTIE: Mother of God, Penelope, it's nearly noon and you're still in your Kimono.

PENNY: Did you eat my Cadbury's nut-milk?

HATTIE: A little nibble. It looked so tempting there behind the clock.

DAVINA: He should be here by now, if the plane was on time.

HATTIE: I've had the fire laid in his bedroom, all he'll have to do is to put a match to it. He'll be feeling the cold dreadfully after the heat of the Tropics.

DAVINA: Where is it you are wishing he has been this time Aunt Hattie?

HATTIE: The Society Islands, I found them on the globe in the Library. Nothing but little specks really, controlled by the French. He may bring us strange shells and pineapples.

CANDY: I shouldn't count on it.

HATTIE: If your Sainted Mother had only lived perhaps he would have wandered less.

DAVINA: One fantasy at a time, Aunt Hattie. Stick to the Society Islands.

HATTIE: Tahiti is one of them. I read it up. Gauguin went there and painted all those brown boneless ladies wearing coloured skirts and no blouses. His visual talent was unparalleled but his character led him to disease and slow destruction. Such a pity.

PENNY: What sort of disease?

HATTIE: The usual social disease that gentlemen acquire in The Society Islands, my darling. Your velvety innocence troubles me at times. Heaven knows you've read enough but I suppose that's not quite the same thing.

DAVINA: Not quite the same thing as what, Aunt Hattie?

HATTIE: The *Sturm und Drang* of actual experience. It's impossible to understand the values of life accurately without a certain amount of personal *Sturm und Drang*.

CANDY: Actual experience isn't always essential to understanding— look at the Brontes.

HATTIE: Ah, those poor sad girls milling about in that meagre little vicarage. They had talent, of course, but at least the ceilings in this house are higher.

DAVINA: We may have talent for all you know, the latent kind that will suddenly burst out of us and astound everybody. We might paint wonderful pictures, write brilliant novels or compose glorious music. It's difficult to tell at our age.

HATTIE: I think there would have been some small indication, some tiny straws in the wind by now, don't you?

PENNY: Candy did that water-colour for you last Christmas and you said it was exquisite.

HATTIE: Honesty is the best policy. The colours were muddy.

CANDY: What about the rhymed epitaph Davina wrote when poor old Twitch died. You said it was profoundly moving.

HATTIE: It didn't scan. I wish you'd change into something more suitable to welcome your father home, Penelope. Only whores wear Kimonos at midday . . . and the Japanese, of course.

(Aunt Hattie goes off to the kitchen)

DAVINA: Poor Aunt Hattie. She's dottier than ever but I'm afraid she's right.

CANDY: What about?

DAVINA: Us not having any talent.

PENNY: Who cares? Talented people lead ghastly lives. They're constantly having to express themselves. They're always a prey to inner conflicts, too. Talent is a hideous responsibility. We're much better off as we are.

DAVINA: How do you mean, "As we are"?

PENNY: Technically virgins but with well raped minds. The written word has seared the scales from our eyes. Nothing will really surprise us now except perhaps sudden love—but that surprises everybody. Lord, the books we've read! If Father had been less impecunious and more responsible and mother hadn't died squeezing me into the world, we might have been educated at Roedean and played Hockey and Lacrosse and lusted after Games mistresses with tiny cavalry moustaches.

CANDY: I don't think I should have somehow. I've searched my heart for lesbian tendencies but in vain. Roedean or no Roedean I shall press on towards some inevitable mate.

DAVINA: I would like all the same to be gifted in some marketable way. Talent with all its defects, can ensure independence.

PENNY: You have beauty, so has Candy. I have something different, but I think it is chemical enough to succeed.

DAVINA: Succeed—succeed in what?

PENNY: Living.

CANDY: I sometimes wish we were Catholics—like Aunt Hattie. It might give us something to hang on to. As it is, owing to Father's lazy Protestantism and mother's fatal lack of education, we're just three merry little agnostics.

PENNY: All dressed up and no place to go.

DAVINA: I think Aunt Hattie's right about that kimono, Penny. It is on the sluttish side. Do go and slip into some Jeans like a good girl.

PENNY: (*Cheerfully*) My bottom's too big for Jeans, but anything to oblige. (*She goes out whistling.*)

CANDY: Penny will always get anything she wants. Her certainty is indestructible.

DAVINA: Perhaps we shall too. I have great hopes.

CANDY: I wish I had. I'm oppressed by doom this morning.

(1962)

How the 'three' ever got 'the money', we shall, sadly, never know.

*   *   *   *

In April 1967 Noël began work on "something quite different". It was to be the last play he was to start and it would be called Age Cannot Wither.

On April 20th he confided to his Diary: *"I have done Act One, Scene One of a new comedy . . . So far it is good and funny, but whether I can keep it up or not remains to be seen. Gone are the days when I could cheerfully polish off a complete play in a few days. Perhaps my standards are higher. At any rate, my impetus has lessened. Not entirely to be wondered at in the late sixties."*

A month later (May 14th): "I have done an act and a half . . . and I am now letting it simmer for a little. I shall probably finish it within the next few weeks." On June 8th he is reflecting that "As far as dialogue is concerned it is very good, but I had a terrible time trying to get the curtain down. Finally, with a scream of relief I managed it and shall now wait until I return from London next week before starting the second act. I have it fairly clearly constructed in my mind so it shouldn't be too difficult."

By the 22nd—"I still haven't embarked on the second act . . . I've been too agitated by everything. I shall get after it when I'm good and ready." The 'everything' included the lingering illness of his secretary, Lorn Loraine; the deaths of old friends, Spencer Tracy and Dorothy Parker; and a particularly irritating film adaptation (Pretty Polly) of one of his short stories. As it turned out, he was never to be 'good and ready'.

Age Cannot Wither *can be seen as a companion piece to* Fallen Angels *(1925). It's as though the earlier play's two heroines—Julia Sterroll and Jane Banbury—had reached the 1960s in their sixties.*

AGE CANNOT WITHER

ACT ONE, SCENE I

The scene is the drawing-room of the Kembles' flat in Bryanston Square. JOHNATHAN *is reading* The Times. NAOMI *is on the telephone.*

NAOMI: Very well then, four-thirty. I shall want Paul for my rinse and Miss Massingham for my nails.—She's away? But she only got back from her holiday two weeks ago—Seaford?—Her mother can't possibly be ill in Seaford, it's supposed to be so bracing.—No, not Miss Churt. She's a sadist, she uses her orange stick like a spear.—What about the dusty looking one with horn-rimmed glasses?—Miss Dadlett. Yes, all right, we'll settle for Miss Dadlett. She's rather inclined to hum little tunes while she's wielding the buffer but perhaps you could warn her in advance that I have no ear for music.— Yes—Four-thirty. Thank you so much. (*She hangs up.*)

JONATHAN: There's been an earthquake in Malta. It lasted for three minutes.

NAOMI: Poor Jane Etheridge.

JONATHAN: What's Jane Etheridge got to do with it?

NAOMI: She lives there, doesn't she?

JONATHAN: The Etheridges are in Gibraltar.

NAOMI: Well, it's the same sort of thing, isn't it? I mean, they're both naval bases. Isn't it time you went to the club? Stella and Judy will be here in a minute.

JONATHAN: I shan't bite them.

NAOMI: You don't like Stella and it's no use pretending you do. You always say she rubs you up the wrong way.

JONATHAN: Judy, on the other hand, always smoothes me down so it levels things out. I'm devoted to Judy, provided she hasn't got that ghastly husband with her.

NAOMI: Robert's all right, so long as you keep him off the Common Market.

JONATHAN: He's a pompous windbag. I can't think why she ever married him in the first place.

NAOMI: The first place was thirty-five years ago. He's probably changed, we're all liable to. I expect he was beautiful as the day and tremendously romantic looking when he was young. I can still see traces of sex-appeal.

JONATHAN: I can't.

NAOMI: It would be most unsuitable if you could.

JONATHAN: When did it actually *start*?

NAOMI: When did *what* actually start?

JONATHAN: This gruesome annual hen-party idea?

NAOMI: Centuries ago, about a month after we'd left St. Ursula's. We all happened to meet by chance at Peter Jones and had lunch together. And it isn't in the least gruesome. It enables us to keep in touch: we reminisce like mad and have a lovely time.

JONATHAN: It seems so set and unspontaneous, like Christmas. I wonder you don't give each other presents.

NAOMI: We do sometimes. A couple of years ago Judy gave me that poodle's head clip with a ruby eye, but the eye fell out and I've never had another one put in.

JONATHAN: It would at least be gracious to wear it. It might encourage her to give you another.

NAOMI: I can't go about wearing a blind poodle.

JONATHAN: I could understand it if you were really close friends, but you barely clap eyes on each other for the rest of the year.

NAOMI: I expect we would if we could, but we all live in different places. Judy's in Paris most of the time, Stella has to stay with Alec in that awful family mausoleum in Perthshire. She only manages to get to London once in every six months.

JONATHAN: We must count our blessings.

NAOMI: I can't think why you're so beastly about poor Stella. She's never done you any harm.

JONATHAN: She's too large and over friendly, like a sheep-dog. I always feel that she expects me to throw a stick for her.

NAOMI: She can't help being large. She never stops doing exercises and dieting. Judy thinks it's glandular. She was always fairly stocky even as a girl.

JONATHAN: I bet the hell she was. She was probably captain of the hockey team as well.

NAOMI: As a matter of fact, she was. She won two silver cups and a complete set of Chaucer in tooled leather.

JONATHAN: Serves her right.

NAOMI: There's time for you to get your hair cut before lunch if you hurry.

JONATHAN: I don't *want* to get my hair cut.

NAOMI: It's getting awfully long at the sides. You don't want to wander about the West End looking scruffy, do you?

JONATHAN: I don't want to wander about the West End anyway, scruffy or not I'm going straight to the club.

NAOMI: Well, what's stopping you?

JONATHAN: Curiosity.

NAOMI: How do you mean, *curiosity*? What are you so curious about?

JONATHAN: I want to see how your old girls are holding up. In comparison with you, I mean.

NAOMI: And how do you think *I'm* holding up?

JONATHAN: Surprisingly well, all things considered.

NAOMI: I can't say I find that 'all things considered' very reassuring. All *what* things considered?

JONATHAN: The March of Time for one. We're none of us getting any younger.

NAOMI: I accept that cliché with the contempt it deserves.

JONATHAN: (*Ignoring her interruption*) Except, of course, Stella. She'll be back in 'rompers' in a couple of years, if she doesn't watch out.

NAOMI: I wish you'd lay off Stella. She seems to be becoming an obsession with you. It's some form of repressed sex-antagonism, I expect. You've probably been secretly in love with her for years without being aware of it. A psychiatrist would put you right in a minute.

JONATHAN: Nonsense.

NAOMI: The subconscious can be more devious than you realise. Ronnie Willford would be a gibbering lunatic at this very minute if he hadn't gone to that man in Mount Street.

JONATHAN: Ronnie Willford will *still* be a neurotic old auntie however many men he went to in Mount Street. I was at Cambridge with him and I know. He had a horrible Siamese cat which bit everybody and he was always fainting in chapel.

NAOMI: The man in Mount Street at least told him what was wrong with him and set him on an even keel.

JONATHAN: Rubbish. All he told him was that he had homosexual tendencies and ought to have a cold bath every morning and go for long walks.

NAOMI: Anyway, he's completely relaxed now and jolly as a sandboy from morning 'till night.

JONATHAN: Jolly *with* a sandboy from morning 'till night is probably nearer the mark.

(STELLA MILVERTON *comes in. She is a heavily-built,
cheerful-looking woman in her sixties*)

STELLA: I stopped Mrs. Rothwell announcing me, because she
            looked flustered. I expect she's got something just coming to
            the boil. (*She kisses* NAOMI *and turns to* JONATHAN) I can't
            think what *you're* doing here, Jonathan. Husbands are strict-
            ly forbidden.

JONATHAN: (*As they shake hands*) I'm leaving immediately.

STELLA: I thought I was going to be late, because Jane rang up in a
            tremendous state of excitement just as I was leaving the
            house. They're going to let her play Paula Tanqueray at the
            next R.A.D.A. matinée!

NAOMI: Surely she's a little young for Paula Tanqueray?

STELLA: They're always too young for everything at the R.A.D.A.
            Last year a girl of fourteen played King Lear. She was quite
            splendid.

NAOMI: Darling Jonathan, as you seem determined to linger on
            where you're not wanted, you might at least make yourself
            useful and mix us a Dry Martini.

JONATHAN: All right. (*He goes to the drink table*)

STELLA: (*Settling herself on the sofa*) I'm bursting with news.

NAOMI: Well, don't say anything important until Judy comes.

STELLA: Oh, nothing world-shattering. Just tit-bits like poor Mona's
            caesarian and that sex-maniac who murdered all those girls
            in Glasgow turning out to be Maisie's cousin.

JONATHAN: Who's Maisie?

STELLA: My new cook. She's gaunt and grey and aggressively
            respectable. You can imagine what a state she's in, poor
            thing.

JONATHAN: Even if she were a fluffy blonde, I should think she'd find
            the situation fairly embarrassing. One doesn't discover a
            murderer in the family every day of the week.

STELLA: She's terrified that she might have to go into the witness box
            and give evidence.

NAOMI: I see her point. I should hate going into a witness box
            myself.

STELLA: It wouldn't be the faintest use if she did anyway. She's a terrible mumbler. I can't understand half of what she's talking about when she's standing bang in front of me.

JONATHAN: *(Handing her a cocktail)* Here's your Martini. I've put in a zest of lemon, is that all right?

STELLA: I'd never say no to a zest of anything. *(She sips it)* It's perfect.

JONATHAN: *(Handing Naomi hers)* Here you are, darling.

NAOMI: Thanks.

JONATHAN: I really am leaving now, so you can begin letting your hair down. Give my love to Judy. *(He blows them a kiss and goes out.)*

STELLA: Dear Jonathan. He always looks so elegant. How on earth does he manage to keep his figure?

NAOMI: He doesn't. He just happens to be made like that. He's terribly lazy and never takes a scrap of exercise.

STELLA: Perhaps he has very small bones.

NAOMI: Possibly, I've never looked.

STELLA: Alec never stops doing exercises. He huffs and puffs for hours every morning. He's even bought one of those idiotic rowing-machines and I have to clamber over it to get into the bath. I wouldn't mind if it did any good but it doesn't. I tried it myself every day for six weeks.

NAOMI: *(Laughing)* Oh, Stella. You must have looked awfully funny!

STELLA: There was no one to see what I looked like. I didn't do it in public.

NAOMI: And there were no results at all?

STELLA: Oh, there were results all right. I felt sick, gave myself a splitting headache and wrenched my shoulder.

NAOMI: Perhaps you could have shots of some sort, why don't you ask your doctor?—you know, hormones and things.

STELLA: No, thank you. Linda Fergurson had hormone injections and grew a black cavalry moustache in under a week.

(MRS. ROTHWELL *flings open the door*)

MRS. R: *(Announcing)* Mrs. Craven.

(JUDY CRAVEN *enters. Of the three ladies she is the most chic. She is expertly dressed, dyed and made-up. Not a hair is out of place.* MRS. ROTHWELL *withdraws, closing the door behind her.*)

JUDY: *(Kissing* NAOMI*)* Dearest Naomi—Here we go again. *(She kisses* STELLA*)* I can hardly believe a year has gone by since last time. It might have been last Tuesday.

NAOMI: *(Admiringly)* Well! I must say you certainly do look ——

JUDY: *(Holding up her hand)* Don't say it. I know perfectly well I look wonderful. If I didn't after all I've been through, I'd shoot myself.

NAOMI: How do you mean—'all you've been through'? *What* have you been through?

JUDY: *(Dramatically)* The full treatment! Face lift, breast lift, the lot. I had to suck Ovaltine through a straw for four whole days. It was hell.

STELLA: You don't mean to say you really—?

JUDY: I certainly do, and what's more I wouldn't go through it again if my chin fell down to my knees. It was perfectly beastly and I loathed every minute of it

STELLA: *(Starry eyed)* You always were the brave one at school. Do you remember striking Miss Lockhart with a hockey stick?

NAOMI: Never mind about Miss Lockhart and hockey sticks for the moment. This is serious. *(To* JUDY*)* When did all this happen? How long ago?

JUDY: Seven months ago. On the fifth of November, as a matter of fact. Gunpowder, treason and plot.

NAOMI: Where?

JUDY: Vienna. It was just one long dreamy waltz.

NAOMI: Why didn't you write and tell us?

JUDY: I wanted it to be a surprise.

STELLA: Well, you got your wish. It most emphatically is.

NAOMI: What did Robert say?

JUDY: He said—'What's the matter, old girl, you look a bit seedy?'

STELLA:	Oh, Judy! How discouraging. After all that trouble!
JUDY:	I suppose it was in a way. Not that I expected him to rush at me in a frenzy of sudden, uncontrolled lust, but I would have liked a casual comment like—'That hat suits you' or 'Your trip to Vienna certainly seems to have done you good.' But not a bit of it. He just went back to his *Times* crossword and asked me for a dismissive verb starting with B in six letters.
STELLA:	I can think of several in four letters.
NAOMI:	Well, all I can say is that I think you've been downright underhand, underhand and crafty.
JUDY:	Believe me, 'understand' is the last word to describe the operation. He snipped and stitched away at me for three and a half hours.
NAOMI:	*Who* did the operation?
JUDY:	Professor Krindling, of course.
NAOMI:	*(Horrified)* Professor Krindling! You must have been mad. He's well known to be the biggest charlatan in the business.
JUDY:	Charlatan or no charlatan, you've got to admit he did a wonderful job on me.
NAOMI:	You took a terrible risk.
JUDY:	Nonsense.
NAOMI:	He was the one who was responsible for Mary Kinnerton's strawberry chin.
JUDY:	Mary Kinnerton's chin was always a worry anyway. Whatever he did to it couldn't have made all that much difference.
STELLA:	Fancy knowing somebody who's actually been to Krindling! What's he like?
JUDY:	Absolutely hideous with tufts of black hair bursting from his ears but gentle as a dove.
NAOMI:	He sounds a horror.
JUDY:	Well, he isn't a horror—he's an angel. And he's an absolute fanatic over his job, a hundred percent dedicated. He used to sit on my bed and tell me the most fascinating things.

You've no idea what you can have done to you nowadays, if you really put your mind to it. You can even have your sex changed at the drop of a hat.

NAOMI: King's Road, Chelsea must be knee deep in discarded bowlers.

JUDY: It's all very fine to laugh and make silly jokes.

NAOMI: I'm not laughing, not really. Actually, I'm thoroughly shocked and horrified. I hate the whole idea of this undignified scampering after Youth. I intend to grow old as gracefully as I can and let nature take its course.

JUDY: Then you'd better give up those blue rinses to start with and eat a lot of chocolate eclairs.

STELLA: *(Laughing)* Touché!

NAOMI: *(Crossly)* I don't know what you mean by 'touché'. I see nothing wrong in trying to make the best of oneself. A little self-discipline never hurt anybody. But I draw the line at plastic surgery, unless it's a medical necessity.

JUDY: Well, I find it a medical necessity to look at least ten years younger than I really am, so you can come off your high horse and stop being so pompous.

NAOMI: I don't mean to be pompous, really I don't. It's just that I can't bear the idea of mutton dressed as lamb.

JUDY: Do you think *I* look like mutton dressed as lamb?

NAOMI: No I can't honestly say that I do. But is it really worth the effort? I mean does it really make you *feel* younger and happier and more able to cope with everything?

JUDY: Yes, it does. It most certainly does.

STELLA: The sad thing about the whole business is that nobody's really fooled.

JUDY: That's not the point. I don't give a hoot whether other people are fooled or not. I shan't care when everybody knows perfectly well that I'm eight-five, so long as I don't *look* it. It's a question of personal satisfaction. I should hate to get out of my bath and look in the glass and see everything hanging about.

NAOMI: Even now there must be a certain amount hanging about.

JUDY: That's just where you're wrong, there isn't, thanks to the dear professor. A snip here and a tuck there have worked wonders. I'll show you if you like.

NAOMI: Not before lunch, dear.

JUDY: Really, Naomi. You should try not to be so prim and hidebound.

NAOMI: It's nothing to do with being prim and hidebound. I just don't want Mrs. Rothwell to come in and see you prancing about stripped to the waist.

JUDY: I hadn't planned on doing the dance of the seven veils.

NAOMI: I also feel that to examine scar-tissue just before Steak Béarnaise might be a bit off-putting.

JUDY: All right—all right—have it your own way. I merely thought you might be interested.

NAOMI: *(Soothingly)* But I *am* interested. I also think it was frightfully brave of you to have it done at all. A little sly perhaps to have been so secretive about it.

JUDY: You could hardly expect me to put an announcement in *The Times*.

STELLA: What I want to know is—did it *hurt*?

JUDY: No, not really. It itched a bit and I felt as if I'd been scalped but it soon wore off. My face swelled up, of course, and looked like a vast Victoria plum for several days. Every time I looked in the glass I got the giggles and that *did* hurt like hell, I must say.

STELLA: Do you think *we* ought to have it done?

NAOMI: What do you mean 'we'? Speak for yourself. Personally, I have no intention of being tampered with.

JUDY: What a ghastly expression. It's only little girls on Wimbledon Common who get tampered with.

STELLA: Oh no, it isn't. Muriel Bailey gets tampered with every time she goes in the tube.

NAOMI: Poor Muriel. She's always been terribly unpunctual. Perhaps that explains it.

STELLA: *(To Judy)* Did you tell Robert you were going to have it done?

JUDY: Of course I told him. I always tell Robert everything.

STELLA: What did he say?

JUDY: 'Anything for a change'!

NAOMI: Has it made any difference to his feeling for you?

JUDY: If by that you mean what I think you mean, you ought to be ashamed of yourself.

NAOMI: I only wondered.

JUDY: Robert and I haven't indulged in any of that sort of thing since nineteen forty-five.

STELLA: Victory year.

JUDY: And we wouldn't have then, if Mrs. Anstruther hadn't been in the Isle of Wight.

NAOMI: That horrible woman! I can never remember her first name.

JUDY: Neither can Robert, I asked him only the other day. He thinks it was Hermione but he wouldn't take a bet on it.

STELLA: Did you mind at the time? About Mrs. Anstruther, I mean?

JUDY: Of course, I did. I was heartbroken. I even hired a private detective to follow them everywhere.

NAOMI: And did he?

JUDY: Yes, but without very satisfactory results. According to his report they went into the New Gallery Cinema and never came out.

STELLA: Perhaps it was *Ben Hur.*

NAOMI: *(With a luxurious sigh)* Isn't it lovely getting old? I wouldn't care now if Jonathan slept with a different woman every night.

JUDY: It's possible that *they* would.

NAOMI: That was a very bitchy thing to say. Jonathan is still a very attractive man.

JUDY: Yes, but not really in that way.

NAOMI: Certainly in 'that way'. He's particularly alluring to the

Young. Debutantes fall for him in droves. Only the other day the eldest Hatherton girl asked him point blank to take her to Paris for the week-end.

JUDY: If he had, I expect 'point blank' would have been the operative phrase.

NAOMI: If you're trying to insinuate ——-

JUDY: I'm not trying to insinuate anything. I'm merely rejecting your fanciful image of dear old Jonathan as a rampaging Casanova. He'll be sixty-eight next birthday. I know that because Robert's is the day before and they always send each other cards.

NAOMI: There's no accounting for the sex-urge. Ninon de l'Enclos went on having lovers until she was pushing ninety.

JUDY: Then she must have been a conceited old ass.

NAOMI: *(Going to the drink table)* Would anyone like another nip?

STELLA: Yes, please. I'm looking forward to the day when I don't have to worry whether I look nice or not.

JUDY: When that day dawns, it will be your last.

STELLA: Do you really think that when I'm a gnarled old crone of ninety-five that I shall still fuss about my hair?

JUDY: Certainly. If you've got any left, and if you haven't, you'll fuss about your wig. Old habits die hard.

STELLA: Oh, God!

JUDY: It's nothing to be depressed about. On the contrary, it shows a certain spiritual nobility. My Aunt Esther died on her eighty-ninth birthday painted up to the eyes.

NAOMI: Had she led a very giddy life?

JUDY: Lord, yes. Three husbands and strings of lovers. One of them was rumoured to be the station-master at Kettering.

STELLA: You mean she was a natural sex-pot?

JUDY: She certainly was. We were none of us allowed to see her until after we'd been confirmed.

STELLA: *(Seriously)* But she really liked sex for sex's sake? I mean it was necessary to her?

JUDY: I suppose it must have been.

STELLA: Well, it isn't to me. It never was.

JUDY: But you must have liked going to bed with people when you were young?

STELLA: I never went to bed with people when I was young. I was occasionally mauled a bit at dances and I once had a set-to with my cousin Stephen in the maze at Hampton Court.

NAOMI: How dreadful. There isn't even anywhere to sit down!

JUDY: All right. We'll settle for the fact that you were a virgin until you married Robert. But what happened then?

STELLA: How do you mean 'what happened then'? The usual thing, I suppose.

JUDY: You were in love with him, weren't you?

STELLA: Of course, I was. I was dotty about him.

JUDY: Then didn't you *enjoy* it?

STELLA: Not at first, I was too agitated. Later on I got sort of used to it. I suppose it *is* rather habit-forming.

JUDY: Oh, Stella—Really!

STELLA: There's no need to look so shocked. I just don't happen to be a voluptuary.

JUDY: It certainly takes more than thirty years of marriage and one set-to in the Hampton Court Maze to make a voluptuary.

STELLA: I really do rather resent your tone of patronage, Judy. We can't all go about swooning over men years younger than we are and working ourselves into states and plunging our heads into gas ovens.

JUDY: It's mean of you to bring that up. It happened years ago and I only put my head in a little way to see what it felt like but it made me sneeze, so I took it out again.

NAOMI: That was Derek What's-his-name, wasn't it?

JUDY: Yes. That was Derek What's-his-name, all right. He certainly was a killer.

NAOMI: He had no back to his head.

JUDY: I never noticed the back of his head. I was always too busy looking at the front. As a matter of fact, I saw him in the Ritz Bar only a few months ago.

STELLA: How did he look?

JUDY: Bright red and bald as an egg.

NAOMI: Oh dear—it does seem sad, doesn't it?

JUDY: Not to me it doesn't. I was absolutely delighted.

NAOMI: Did you see who was with him?

JUDY: Not very clearly. They were right at the other end of the bar near the door.

NAOMI: Perhaps it was Mildred.

JUDY: Not unless she's recently joined the Navy.

NAOMI: *(Fascinated)* Oooh, just fancy! Derek of all people. Upper deck or lower?

JUDY: Upper, but only just.

STELLA: It's no surprise to me, I always had my suspicions about Derek. There was something in the way he played the piano.

JUDY: Come now, Stella. He did at least play the piano beautifully.

STELLA: Too much Debussy.

NAOMI: None of the men in my life have been able to play a note on anything. Jonathan did buy a ukelele soon after we were married but it gave him a blister on his thumb and he threw it into the fire.

STELLA: Like that beastly roman Emperor and those little boys.

JUDY: What on earth are you talking about?

STELLA: I can't remember his name off hand but I know he used to throw little boys into the fire after he'd had his way with them.

JUDY: Italians are naturally cruel, I'm afraid. Look how they whack away at those wretched donkeys in Capri.

STELLA: This drink's terribly strong. If lunch doesn't happen soon, I shall fall down.

NAOMI: It should be ready any minute.

JUDY: Couldn't you ring a bell or something?

NAOMI: Good Heavens, no. Mrs. Rothwell would have a fit. She's terribly highly-strung.

JUDY:	One should never allow oneself to be dominated by servants.
NAOMI:	That feudal attitude won't wash nowadays, Judy. If anything upset Mrs. Rothwell, I should be done for. Also, when the bell rings in the kitchen, it really is deafening. Enough to give anyone a nervous breakdown.
JUDY:	That could be fixed by wedging in a bit of rag.
NAOMI:	Then it wouldn't ring at all, so we should be back where we started.
STELLA:	Wouldn't it be awful if we really were?
JUDY:	Really were *what*?
STELLA:	Back where we started. On the threshold of life—young and eager and oversexed.
NAOMI:	Speak for yourself. I wasn't oversexed.
JUDY:	What about Miss Mowforth? You were barmy about her.
NAOMI:	That had nothing to do with sex, it was a spiritual relationship.
JUDY:	You kept a snapshot of her in fencing-bloomers in your handkerchief drawer.
NAOMI:	What about you and Doctor Pringle? I remember you fainting dead away when he sounded your chest.
JUDY:	That wasn't passion. I was sickening for mumps.
STELLA:	You were too old for mumps.
JUDY:	Nevertheless, I had them all right. Is mumps them or it?
NAOMI:	It must be them. You can't have a mump all by itself.
STELLA:	Isn't it lucky that we're all reasonably healthy? Considering our ages I mean.
JUDY:	I'm not reasonably healthy. I'm a martyr to practically everything. I cough and sniffle from November to May and in June I get hay fever, which torments me until the end of September.
NAOMI:	At least you have October to look forward to.
STELLA:	(*Earnestly*) I still maintain that we're fantastically lucky. We might be bed-ridden or crippled with arthritis or bent double like croquet-hoops. Instead we're all three sound in

wind and limb and ready for anything.

JUDY: You always exaggerate so. We're far from being ready for anything, except lunch. And it doesn't look as if we're ever going to get that.

NAOMI: You must be patient, it's a cheese soufflé. She couldn't possibly start it until you'd both got here. You might have been stuck in a traffic jam and it would have sunk like a stone. Would you like another little nip?

JUDY: If I had another little nip I shouldn't be able to tell the difference between a cheese soufflé and a steak and kidney pudding.

STELLA: At least nothing agitating is likely to happen to any of us now, we're too old. Except getting ill and dying, of course.

JUDY: Do stop harping on how old we are. It's undermining. I'm beginning to feel as though I couldn't get out of this chair without help.

NAOMI: I doubt if you can. It's a perfect beast, like a hip-bath. Even quite young people get stuck in it.

STELLA: I'd hate to get ill but I don't believe I shall mind dying all that much.

JUDY: It's easy enough to say that now but just you wait until the time comes. You'll probably be in the most awful frizz.

STELLA: I don't know why you should assume that. Lots of people are calm as cucumbers on their death beds and think up lovely memorable things to say to comfort everybody.

JUDY: I doubt if I shall. I'm more likely to be in a tearing rage and insult people right and left.

NAOMI: *(Thoughtfully)* I shall cry, I expect. Not the boo-hooing, snuffly kind of crying, but just gentle, helpless tears, because everyone is being so kind to me.

JUDY: Perhaps they won't be.

NAOMI: Of course they will. People are always kind at death beds. They smooth your pillows and keep putting their fingers to their lips and tip-toeing about the darkened room.

JUDY: That would drive me mad to start with.

STELLA: Why don't we change the subject to something more cheerful? Lunch, for instance.!

NAOMI: I wish you'd shut up about lunch. It'll be ready in a minute.

STELLA: I'm famished and it's nearly a quarter to two.

JUDY: Perhaps Mrs. Rothwell has had some sort of accident.

NAOMI: Mrs. Rothwell could never have an accident. You only have to look at her.

STELLA: I wish I could look at her. I've never wanted to look at anybody so much in my life.

JUDY: Three grandmothers! It really does seem grotesque, doesn't it? Almost indecent.

NAOMI: What's indecent about it? I don't know what you mean.

JUDY: The way we behave and dress and carry on. It's all so unsuitable somehow.

STELLA: What on earth are you talking about?

JUDY: I think nineteenth century grandmothers were far more attractive and impressive than twentieth century ones. they were yellowish and frail and infinitely more understanding and smelt vaguely of lavender water.

STELLA: Mine didn't. She had a voice like a fog-horn and smelt dreadful.

NAOMI: What of?

STELLA: Moth balls, principally, but there was something else as well, I can't quite describe it —

JUDY: Well, be a dear and don't try.

NAOMI: Actually, I do rather see what Judy means. Nobody seems o get comfortably old any more. I'm sure we should all three of us find life far less agitating if we'd given up at fifty and were content to sit about clanking with cameo brooches.

JUDY: Old and gray and full of sleep and nodding by the fire.

STELLA: I'd rather sit in Antoine's, where at least there's someone to nod to.

JUDY: I still maintain that we present the wrong image.

STELLA: Who to?

JUDY: The world in general and our grandchildren in particular.

How can we expect them to rush to us with their tiny troubles when we're always having our hair set and our nails done?

STELLA: You're getting your generations mixed, dear. My granddaughter's last tiny trouble had to be dealt with by that very dubious doctor in St. John's Wood.

NAOMI: Jennifer *is* an exception, Stella. You must admit that.

STELLA: I don't admit anything of the sort. The majority of the Young today are morally irresponsible. Jennifer was just a bit careless. She was always vague as a child.

NAOMI: I think to become pregnant at the age of eighteen and a half is carrying vagueness a little too far.

JUDY: She inherits a lot of it from her mother.

STELLA: I resent that, Judy. Harriet was a bit forgetful, I agree, but she had a brilliant mind.

JUDY: She left two bull terrier puppies in the ladies lavatory at Paddington. If that isn't vague I should like to know what is.

NAOMI: Oh, poor things! What happened to them?

JUDY: The usual routine. Lost Property Office, Battersea Dogs' Home, advertisements in *The Daily Telegraph*. She got them back eventually.

NAOMI: Thank God for that. I can't bear to think of dogs being left about and forsaken. They must suffer so dreadfully not being able to explain anything to anybody.

STELLA: I don't suppose abandoned babies on doorsteps have too good a time, either.

NAOMI: At least they don't run the risk of being put into strange kennels and getting bitten by other abandoned babies.

STELLA: I don't care what you say about us presenting the wrong image, Judy. I still think we have every reason to congratulate ourselves.

JUDY: What on earth for?

STELLA: *(Vehemently)* Because we've survived! We've cleared all the hazards and hurdles and ditches. All we have to do now is to canter serenely down the home stretch.

NAOMI: Your phraseology is over-ebullient, Stella, it always was. We're none of us capable of cantering anywhere. It's as much as I can do to stagger from the top of Sloane Street to Harrods.

STELLA: You know perfectly well what I mean. We've all three of us been through the mill in our different ways and at last, at long last, we can afford to put our feet up and relax. There really isn't much that can happen to us now.

JUDY: For God's sake, touch wood!

STELLA: I wouldn't dream of touching wood. In my opinion all those foolish old superstitions encourage disaster rather than prevent it.

NAOMI: That's a superstition in itself.

STELLA: I don't in the least mind being thirteen at table and I can't wait to walk under ladders.

NAOMI: I'm afraid you'll have to until after lunch. Unless I can persuade Mrs. Rothwell to set up the kitchen steps outside the dining-room door.

(MRS. ROTHWELL *enters*)

MRS. R.   (*Announcing*) Luncheon is served, Madame.

(MRS. ROTHWELL *withdraws leaving the door open.*
NAOMI *ushers the others out.*)

(1967)

*   *   *   *

And on what better line could one wish to exit?

I-2-11

IRENE: Quite frankly — I don't.

LESTER: Well — sort of remote, you know — shut up like a box.

IRENE: That sounds dreamy — I can't wait.

LESTER: But if you draw him out a bit he's sheer heaven.

LUELLA: In what way? Come on, darling — give — for God's sake — we're all on tenterhooks.

LESTER: Well he's quiet and quite witty at moments — dry you know.

IRENE: Well, I suppose that's better than being wet.

LESTER: I can see that Irene's got a thing against him before she's even seen him.

LUELLA: She's been anti-British for the last six months — it's only because she takes the Post instead of the Sun.

LESTER: Well, he's a brilliant writer — you can't get away from that.

IRENE: I intend to get away from it as fast as ever I can.

DWIGHT: What's the guy written?

LUELLA: His last book — 'A London Lady' — was a best seller. It was about the English Restoration — you know — Charles the Second. It was quite good.

IRENE: Like 'Forever Amber.'

LUELLA: No — I will say that for it — it was <u>not</u> like 'Forever Amber.'

IRENE: What does he look like?

Manuscript page for Long Island Sound *(1947), an unproduced play based on his short story, "What Mad Pursuit".*

I TRAVEL ALONE

I travel alone,
Sometimes I'm East,
Sometimes I'm West,
No chains can ever bind me;
No remembered love can ever find me;
I travel alone.

("I Travel Alone")

IN REALITY ONE OF THE VERY FEW TIMES NOËL TRAVELLED ALONE WAS ON HIS first impoverished trip to New York in 1921. Thereafter, despite his insistence in songs like "World Weary" that he could hardly wait to see great open spaces --which he would prefer to observe without the benefit of his "loving friends"—he was almost always accompanied by Jeffrey Amherst, Jack Wilson, Cole Lesley, Graham Payn or some other member of the 'family'.

There were very few great open spaces in the New York of 1921 and its impact on the young Noël was immediate and lasting—so much so that he determined to commit his impressions of this "marvellous party" to a tongue-in-cheek 'American Diary' . . .

"My publisher has informed me that it is the note of careless intimacy in published diaries which attracts the public. According to him, people love to know a bit about names and personalities that they have never met. For instance, if I wrote—"Tuesday—met Mrs. Fiske—how like she is to Auntie Clara, only without her nose"—everyone would be immensely thrilled. Tho' until that moment they had never heard of Auntie Clara, they would experience a pleasant glow of satisfaction in the thought of how like she was to Mrs. Fiske. An atmosphere of charming cameraderie would be established. Mrs. Fiske would in all probability receive heaps of letters likening her to their Auntie Jessie's and their Auntie Amy's and everyone would be pleased.

I was awfully thrilled when he suggested a diary of my American visit. Here is the opportunity I have been waiting for, I told myself. I shall be able to be frightfully witty and everybody will talk a lot about my caustic pen, etc. I shall tell the true story of Mrs. Vernon Ball and the Parrot . . . and I shan't scruple to publish the facts of the Southampton weekend party when Mrs. Frazzle and Marie Prune did that most peculiar nautch dance in their bathing dresses.

I rushed back to the Brevort Hotel trembling with the news. Lester Donahue was practising when I burst in and told him. "I have been asked to write an intimate diary of my American visit", I cried. Lester gave me a dreadful look, shut the piano and left the country.

NEW YORK DIARY

SATURDAY
"I felt that some sort of scene was necessary to celebrate my first entrance into America, so I said—'Little lamb, who made thee?' to a Customs official. A fracas far exceeding my wildest dreams ensued, during which he delved down with malice aforethought to the bottom of my trunk and discovered the oddest things in my sponge bag. I think I'm going to like America. I have very good letters to frightfully influential people—Daniel Blood, Dolores Harper, Senator Pinchbeck, Violet Curyon Meyer and Julia Pescod—so I ought to get along all right socially at any rate.

WEDNESDAY
For a really jolly evening I recommend the Times Square subway station. You get into any train with that delicious sensation of breathless uncertainty as to where you are going. To ask an official is sheer folly, as any tentative question is calculated to work them up to a frenzy of rage and violence. To ask your fellow passengers is equally useless, as they are generally as dazed as you are. The great thing is to keep calm and at all costs to avoid Expresses. As another means of locomotion the Elevated Railway possesses a rugged charm. The serene pleasure of gazing into frowsy bedroom windows at elderly coloured ladies in bust

bodices and flannel petticoats is only equalled by the sudden thrill you experience when the two front carriages hurtle down to the street in flames.

This morning I took two of my plays to Fred Latham at the Globe Theatre. He didn't accept them for immediate production but told me of two delightful bus rides—one going up Riverside Drive and the other coming down Riverside Drive. I was very grateful, as the buses this slow moving are more or less tranquil and filled with the wittiest advertisements, which make everyone rock with laughter

THURSDAY

Spent all last night at Coney Island. I've never known such an atmosphere of genuine carnival. We went on The Whip, the sudden convulsions of which drove the clasp of my braces sharply into my back, scarring me, I think, for life. Now I know why Americans always wear belts.

Then we went into a Haunted House, where a board gave way beneath my foot and nicked my ankle. The Giant Dipper was comfortingly tame, as I only bruised my side and cut my cheek—after which we had 'Hot Dog and Stout', which the others seemed to enjoy immensely. Then—laughing gaily—we all ran through a revolving wooden wheel. At least, the others did. I inadvertently caught my foot and fell, which caused a lot of amusement. I shall not go out again with a sharp cigarette case in my pocket."

MONDAY, 23RD

Met AW (Alexander Woollcott) at a first night. We were roguish together for hours and I liked him enormously. What a pity he's so devoted to Marnie Prune—not that I actually dislike her but, really, a woman of her age ought never to behave in such an abandoned manner. Also that dreadful blouse she wore made me feel quite ill and she squinted vilely.

I went on afterwards to 'Montmartre'. Ina Claire was there looking lovely as usual—anyhow she's one of the cleverest artistes in the world. I noticed poor Vera Frazzle at the next table. She was rather drunk and obviously upset about her sister running away with a Chinaman. After all, who wouldn't be?

THURSDAY, 31ST

Just back from a weekend at Southampton with Mrs. Vernon Bale— what a charming woman she is and such a rascal! We played the most peculiar games on Sunday evening and she and Florrie Wick did a nautch dance which was most bizarre and entertaining—how hospitable Americans are! I've fixed up heaps of luncheon engagements for next week. Edgar Poophatch was particularly kind. He offered to introduce me to Carl Van Veethien and Sophie Tucker, both of whom I've been longing to meet.

SATURDAY, 4TH

Met the Theatre Guild and played Hide and Seek with them in the park. Helen Westley fell into the pond—how we laughed. Lunched at the Algonquin with the *crème de la crème* of the artistic world. Francis Carson, George Kaufman and notably, Cynthia Burdleheim, who ate her food quite disgustingly and was wearing imitation pearls the size of hen's eggs. Later on we went and had tea at Mesa Malmean's Studio, which was most attractive. She is a perfect hostess and there was an air of pleasing bohemianism about the whole affair which went far towards making me take another cake. In more formal circumstances I should naturally have refrained. After tea I played the piano and sang and everybody talked—mostly while I was singing. It was all great fun.

TUESDAY, 7TH

Such a busy day—had a play refused by William Harris and this book turned down by Scribner's. I also fell off the bus, being unused to getting off on the right hand side. I just love America.

SUNDAY, 16TH

If I had money, I should buy the English rights of *Dulcy*. I went to the first night with Alfred Lunt—it's wonderfully good and Lynn Fontanne is brilliant. I remember she was always clever even playing small parts in London years ago. America is the place to get on. I had this book refused by Harcourt Brace only yesterday . . . I should always like to have a little working model of Broadway at night—just to take out and look at when I feel depressed. I'm quite sure it is one of the most amazing sights in the world. I shall feel awfully offended for Piccadilly Circus when I get back."

*   *   *   *

For the mature Noël his respite from the pressures that came with early and repeated success was to 'sail away' and he saw the world several times over in the late 1920s and 30s. In the course of his travels he came to define for himself his personal safe haven—a compound of all the places he had liked. He called it—Samolo.

Samolo was the mythical South Sea island he first created for "We Were Dancing", one of the plays in the 1936 Tonight At 8:30 *sequence. It caught his imagination, because it could be anything he wanted it to be and by the time he came to visit it again in* Pacific 1860, *he had defined it more clearly . . .*

Graham Payn recalls going down to White Cliffs, Noël's weekend retreat in Kent, one weekend in 1945 "to find him and Cole Lesley poring over the 'authorised' map of Samolo. They'd already worked out details of climate, topography and a brief historical outline as well as a basic Samolan vocabulary."

"Samolo is the principal island of the Samolan archipelago in the South-Western Pacific.

Latitude: 18 degrees North. Longitude: 175 degrees West.

The Samolan group consisting of 34 islands (seven of which are inhabited and a few privately owned) was discovered in 1786 by Captain Evangelous Cobb.

The first English missionaries appeared there in 1814.

Christianity was adopted by the Samolans in 1815 during the reign of King Kefumalani.

The islands became officially a British possession in 1855 during the reign of King Kefumalani II, who wrote personally to Queen Victoria, begging her to allow his land to have the privilege of belonging to the British Empire.

The first British Governor-General of Samolo was Sir Douglas Markham, K.C.B., 1855.

In the eighteen-sixties, the British population of the islands numbered approximately one thousand four hundred. Sir Lewis Grayshott had succeeded Sir Douglas Markham as Governor-General.

The island of Samolo is of volcanic origin and is 108 miles long and 70 miles wide.

The headland is rough and barren with black rocks and a profusion of sea-birds including albatrosses, which "indulge much in curious dances two by two."

(Extract from A Guide to Samolo, published by Ross, Wishart & Sons, 1906)

*   *   *   *

In the 1951 play South Sea Bubble *he was back again, this time in the present tense, pillorying the pretension of the British colonials and their refusal to face the fact of change.*

In a fragment of an unfinished novel, A Summer's Cloud—*written at about this time—his two leading characters Robin and 'Grizel' Craigie return to Samolo after a year's leave and Grizel, at least, bleakly observes a few modern 'improvements' in the old place . . .*

"Samolo, when I had left it eleven months before, had still been relatively true to its reputation as one of the few unspoiled islands in the Pacific but even then it had begun to quiver a bit under the implacable hand of 'progress'. Milk bars appeared in all sorts of unlikely places and ugly black aerials like toasting-forks began to disfigure the roofs of native houses, even in the country districts.

When I returned I observed sadly that the rot had spread with dreadful swiftness. The lovely grove of Royal Palms just outside Pendaria on the Narouchi road had been cut down to make room for an 'Odeon', which looked like a vast green blancmange and was even more eye-searing in the evening when its entire hideous facade was outlined in shrieking blue neon lights. A new apartment building, resembling a gargantuan slice of wedding cake, had sprung up on the Western tip of Paiana Bay, dwarfing everything within an area of several miles and completely obscuring the sunset from all the houses on that particular stretch of coast. There was also, slap in the middle of King Street, an immense Department Store on every floor of which radios blasted at full pitch making it impossible to buy a tube of Kolynos without having a nervous breakdown."

*   *   *   *

We next meet the Craigies in Noël's only published novel, Pomp and Circumstance *(1960) and it is roughly at this point that one senses that his fictional Shangri-la has merged with his real life one and Samolo has become a synonym for—Jamaica.*

He visited Jamaica for much needed recuperation at the very end of

the war on instructions from his Intelligence boss, Sir William "Little
Bill" Stephenson and fell in love with it on sight.

By the early 1950s he has bought and built a home there and he would
spend at least part of every year on the then unspoiled island. While he was
looking for a suitable property or plot of land, he rented Ian Fleming's
house, 'Goldeneye'. He considered the weekly rental of £50 exorbitant, in
view of the marked lack of creature comforts, and put his feelings into
verse, once he was safely home . . .

HOUSE GUEST

Alas! I cannot adequately praise
The dignity, the virtue and the grace
Of this most virile and imposing place
Wherein I passed so many airless days.

Alas! I cannot accurately find
Words to express the hardness of the seat
Which, when I cheerfully sat down to eat,
Seared with such cunning into my behind.

Alas! However much I raved and roared,
No rhetoric, no witty diatribe
Could ever, even partially, describe
The impact of the spare-room bed—and board.

Alas! Were I to write 'till crack of doom
No typewriter, no pencil, nib nor quill
Could ever recapitulate the chill
And arid vastness of the living-room.

Alas! I am not someone who exclaims
With rapture over ancient equine prints.
Ah no, dear Ian, I can only wince
At *all* those horses framed in *all* those frames.

Alas! My sensitivity rebels,
Not at loose shutters, not at a plague of ants

Nor other 'sub-let' bludgeonings of chance,
But at those hordes of ageing, fading shells.
Alas! If only commonsense could teach
The stubborn heart to heed the cunning brain,
You would, before you let your house again,
Remove the barracudas from the beach.

But still, my dear Commander, I admit,
No matter how I criticise and grouse
That I was strangely happy in your house—
In fact I'm very, very fond of it..

Many of the fictional events in Pomp and Circumstance *can now be seen to have their origins in Jamaica's real life goings on in those years.*

Much of the plot has to do with Eloise, Duchess of Fowey, sneaking off to Samolo to dally with Bunny Collins, a bachelor who is most distinctly not gay, though extremely lively, while the Craigies have to provide 'cover' for these impetuous middle-aged lovers.

A little earlier in Jamaica Fleming has been conducting a comparable affair with Ann, Lady Rothermere, wife of the press baron and Ian's boss. A tricky business at best, complicated by the fact of Rothermere's deadly rival, Lord Beaverbrook, happening to live round the corner. Noël & Co. were frequently required to act as go-betweens and it was a considerable relief when, in 1952, for good or ill—Ann and Ian became one.

The nuptials allowed Noël to commemorate their belated marital commitment in another verse . . .

DON'TS FOR MY DARLINGS

The quivering days of waiting
Of wondering and suspense
Without regret can at least be set
In the Past Imperfect tense.
The agonies and frustrations,
The blowing now cold, now hot,
Are put to rest, and there's no more doubt
As to whether you will or not.
The overly publicised secret

We all of us knew so well
Lo and behold, can at last be told
To the sound of a marriage bell.
All the stories that could be written,
The legends the world could spin
Of those turbulent years you've lived, my dears,
In excessively open sin.
Permit me as one who adores you,
An eminent *éminence grise*,
To help you in finding some method of minding
Your marital Qs and Ps
Don't, Ian, if Annie should cook you
A dish that you haven't enjoyed,
Use that as excuse for a storm of abuse
Of Anna or Lucien Freud.
Don't, Annie, when playing canasta
Produce a lipstick from your 'sac'
And drop your ace with a roguish grimace
While giving dear Delia the pack.
Don't Ian, when guests are arriving
By aeroplane, motor or train
Retire to bed with a cold in the head
And that ever redundant migraine.
Don't be too exultant, dear Annie,
Restrain all ebullient *bons mots*,
The one thing that vexes the old boy's old Ex's
Is knowing the status is quo
Don't either of you, I implore you,
Forget that one truth must be faced -
Although you may measure repentance at leisure -
You HAVEN'T been married in haste.

*   *   *   *

But the story was far from over. While Ann was conducting her courting commuting between Jamaica and England, it appears that Ian was not inclined to live the life celibate

In 1957—in an unpublished play, Volcano—*art copied life once more. Adela (Blanche), an attractive middle-aged widow keeps a hotel in the shadow of the island's supposedly dormant volcano, Fumfumbolo. She has just broken off an ill-judged affair with the local lothario, Guy (Ian)—when Guy's wife, Melissa (Ann) arrives to assess the seriousness of the latest competition . . .*

VOLCANO

MELISSA: You met at a Government House cocktail party or something, didn't you?

ADELA: Yes, quite casually. It was later on that we became really close friends.

MELISSA: You're very fond of him, aren't you?

ADELA: Yes, I am. Tremendously fond of him.

MELISSA: He's not really a frightfully satisfactory person to be 'tremendously' fond of. But I expect you've already found that out for yourself.

ADELA: No. As a matter of fact, I haven't yet.

MELISSA: Well, I'm sure I hope you never will. I have a feeling that Guy wasn't particularly eager for me to come out here.

ADELA: Really? What makes you think that?

MELISSA: Nothing tangible. Merely that I feel he regards this island as his own special pigeon, his own private bachelor paradise.

ADELA: Nevertheless, you came, didn't you? In spite of your nightmare and presentiments about flying, you made the journey.

MELISSA: Yes. I always make the journey. *(She laughs)* It's becoming monotonous.

ADELA: *(Equably)* Oh, surely not? To see with one's eyes, to find out for oneself may be agitating perhaps, or painful, or even shocking, but not monotonous.

MELISSA: It is if one always finds out the same thing.

ADELA: *(Challenging)* The same thing?

MELISSA: *(Looking her square in the eye)* Yes, Adela. Exactly the same thing.

ADELA: I'm not quite sure that I know what we're talking about.

MELISSA: *(Lightly)* Oh, aren't you? How disappointing. I thought we both knew and were handling it rather well.

ADELA: *(Directly)* Yes, Melissa. You are quite right. We *do* know. Whether we're handling it so well or not remains to be seen—I hope you're right about that, too.

MELISSA: Perhaps later on, when we know each other a little better, we shall find it easier to decide. In the meantime I suppose the only thing for us to do is to press on.

ADELA: I assure you that I'm more than willing.

MELISSA: *(With a smile)* Yes. Curiously enough, I know you are.

ADELA: You're not really like I imagined you'd be either.

MELISSA: Why do you say that?

ADELA: I didn't expect you to be so—vulnerable.

MELISSA: I suspect that we're both a little more vulnerable than we pretend to be. It's a good thing really, I think, to preserve a reasonable façade. I can't bear women who go through life dangling their hearts from their sleeves like charm bracelets.

ADELA: *(Laughing)* I quite agree.

MELISSA: Things are looking up a bit, aren't they?

ADELA: Yes. I really believe they are

In the play Melissa finally decides that enough is enough and departs, leaving the field clear for Adela, who then makes it clear that she no longer wants it either. Guy is left pathetically pleading—a reflection of Noël's by now considerable disenchantment with Fleming's self-indulgence.

ADELA *settles herself in a long chair under the lamp and lights a cigarette.*
GUY *comes up the steps from the garden. He is not in the least drunk,*
but he has been drinking.)

GUY: I thought they'd never go.

ADELA: *(Looking up a trifle startled)* Guido!

GUY: I've been hiding behind that hibiscus hedge for ages.

ADELA: *(Rising)* What on earth for?

GUY: I wanted to see you.

ADELA: I would be equally discernible if you came in by the front door.

GUY: I've come to say goodbye. I'm leaving tomorrow.

ADELA: Yes, I know you are.

GUY: *(Handing her a small basket of shells)* I've brought you these. To add to your collection.

ADELA: How very sweet of you. They're lovely. *(SHE examines them)* They're not from here?

GUY: No. Since Melissa went home I've been doing a little island hopping. I borrowed old Papalai's schooner. He and his son sailed it and I lay about and watched the flying-fish. These actually came from Toongpalo. There's a superb beach right at the Northernmost tip of the island, you can only get to it through a small cut in the reef. I'll take you next year, if you'll come.

ADELA: It sounds enchanting.

GUY: Will you—will you come?

ADELA: *(Lightly)* Certainly. Why shouldn't I?

GUY: You've gone an awfully long way away.

ADELA: Don't be silly.

GUY: Has that molten lava destroyed everything? Shrivelled up even your ordinary affection for me?

ADELA: I didn't know you were interested in ordinary affection.

GUY: I'm humbly grateful for anything I can get.

ADELA: What do you hope to get?

GUY: Please forgive me, Adela. I can't go away tomorrow and leave you hating me so coldly.

ADELA: I don't hate you.

GUY: Only two weeks ago you said, here on this very verandah, that you loved me.

ADELA: Was that only two weeks ago? How extraordinary.

GUY: *(Pleadingly)* Adela . . . *(He takes her in his arms and kisses her passionately.* SHE *stands quite still, making no effort at resistance. Presently he stops and steps back from her.)*

ADELA: *(Levelly)* Perhaps you'd like a drink?

GUY: *(Staring at her)* No, thank you.

ADELA: Then don't you think you'd better go now? There's a
           banana boat in tomorrow, which means that I have to get up
           very early in the morning—and I'm rather tired.

GUY: *(In a low voice)* I want you, Adela. I want to make love to you.

ADELA: Yes, Guido. I gathered that.

GUY: And you want me to, don't you—in your heart" In spite of
           everything that has happened, I know you do. I can feel it.

ADELA: Oh, Guido. How can you be so intolerably stupid! It's too
           shaming.

GUY: Is it so shaming—to be told that you're desired?

ADELA: In these circumstances—yes—very.

GUY: Can circumstances change so completely, so utterly, in two
           short weeks?

ADELA: *(Curiously)* Did you seriously believe, when you came here
           tonight, that we could be lovers again?

GUY: I hoped, so very much, that we might?

ADELA: Why?

GUY: I've already told you—I want you.

ADELA: And you really think that is enough reason?

GUY: It's all right. I see now that I was wrong. I apoligise.

ADELA: I don't want your apologies. Please go away and leave me
           alone.

GUY: Adela—

ADELA: You have an exaggerated view of your own personal charm,
           Guido, you're over-confident. But there are a few people in
           life, and I am one of them, for whom even the most potent
           charm is not enough. I once read somewhere long ago that
           the most important thing in human existence was the capac-
           ity for loving. You, it seems, only have the capacity for grab-
           bing what you want and possessing it. There's a whole world
           of difference between the two. You wreak a great deal of
           havoc, swaggering through women's lives, looting and plun-
           dering and winning your easy victories, but later on, when

the years begin to close in on you and you find yourself alone on your empty, desolate battlefield, perhaps you'll realise how pitifully little you had to offer them. Please go now.

GUY: *(After a pause)* I know I've behaved vilely. I know I've forfeited every right to your forgiveness, even your tolerance. But still I beg you for it, if only for old time's sake.

ADELA: It doesn't become you to beg, Guido. I'd rather you sailed out of my life under the skull and crossbones than under a pallid flag of truce.

GUY: Am I really to sail out of your life—permanently?

ADELA: Of course.

GUY: *(After another pause)* Then there's nothing more to be said, is there?

ADELA: *(Smiling)* Nothing at all. Except perhaps—"Bon Voyage".

(GUY *looks at her hopelessly for a moment.* SHE *stands immovable, the empty smile still on her face, while he goes slowly down the steps and into the garden. When* HE *has gone the smile fades, leaving her face quite expressionless.* SHE *moves over to the table on which she has placed the basket of shells, and, taking them out of the basket one by one, she smashes them violently on the ground.)*

THE CURTAIN FALLS

*   *   *   *

There was to be one more literary return to the islands . . .

Noël left behind a draft manuscript for an uncompleted novel, Beyond These Voices, *though there is no indication as to when it was written. It is set in Samolo in the late 1950s and reads more elegaically than* Pomp and Circumstance—*almost as though both the writer and the narrator, Kerry Stirling, were taking their leave . . .*

It begins . . .

"I have come home again, this time, I suspect, for good. The years that are left to me I intend to pass here on the island where the winds are soft and the climate temperate and where, except for a few weeks twice a year in the rainy season, there is always sunshine."

This thought fills me with gentle pleasure for I am tired. Not physically tired, for I am in the best of health and look and feel a great deal younger than I am, but spiritually a little under the weather. This is not a disagreeable sensation; on the contrary it is rather pleasant, for there is space around me and time ahead of me, time enough at least to enable me to give myself up to my quiet *malaise* and wait, without agitation, until the unhurried days smooth it away."

By the time he arrived in Jamaica that last time, there were, as it turned out, only days left to Noël. He died peacefully in the early morning of March 26th, 1973.

And, indeed, the winds that day were soft . . .